F

MW01247936

FIGHTING FOR LIFE

Stories from the Past
With Lessons for the Present

GARY M. McNALLY

I

Dedication

For the Greatest Generation, whose heroic courage and endurance saved nations.

And for Janine, Hannah, Jonathan, and Jami, who know something of what it means to suffer as soldiers of Christ and who mean more to me than life itself.

FIGHTING FOR LIFE

*"For we do not wrestle against flesh and blood,
but against principalities, against powers,
against the rulers of the darkness of this age...
Therefore, take up the whole armor of God,
that you may be able to withstand in the evil day,
and having done all, to stand."*
Ephesians 6:12 (NKJV).

CONTENTS

Preface

*"Now, when he [David] had finished speaking to Saul,
the soul of Jonathan was knit to the soul of David,
and Jonathan loved him as his own soul."*
1 Samuel 18:1 (NKJV).

Winston Churchill once said, "All the great things are simple, and many can be expressed in a single word: freedom, justice, honor, duty, mercy, hope."

I would suggest that the first word, "freedom," beats strongest in the heart of most men. Throughout human history, men have willingly sacrificed their lives in the service of and the quest for freedom. As Americans, the love of freedom seems to be in our DNA. When it is lost, we cry out for it. When tyrants would take it away, we fight to our last breath to retain it.

Some of the strongest bonds in life are formed among men who have shared the experience of war. If we didn't already know that, the miniseries *Band of Brothers* taught us so.

In these forty devotional readings, I have tried to highlight some obvious parallels between physical and spiritual warfare. Less obvious is the idea that both share a common motivation:

the quest for freedom. In physical warfare, the quest is to be free from earthly tyranny and oppression. In spiritual warfare, the quest is to be free from spiritual interference and oppression.

I believe that the moment in history recorded for us in 1 Samuel 17-18 is the ultimate example of the melding of the two. A short time before David met the Philistine giant, Goliath, in the Valley of Elah, Jonathan had attacked and single-handedly eliminated 20 Philistine soldiers (1 Samuel 14) near Michmash on the Central Benjamin Plateau. I have visited the location where this incident occurred. Just seeing the setting and what it would have taken to climb into position is daunting enough, never mind actually making the attack.

Clearly, the Lord was with Jonathan in a powerful way, just as He was with David when he fought Goliath. Both men were obviously very physically capable, but more importantly, both were men who had a deep and abiding relationship with their Lord. When Jonathan witnessed David's slaying of Goliath, an unshakable bond was formed between the two.

Both Jonathan and David would spend their remaining days defending their earthly freedom and fighting Israel's earthly enemies. But of first importance is the fact that both would do so while striving for ever greater spiritual freedom here, which would increasingly whet their appetite for eternal freedom hereafter.

This is my prayer for you, the reader, the soldier, the warrior. Fight the earthly battles for freedom that are justified, but do so while giving first priority to your quest for spiritual and eternal freedom.

If you are currently serving or are a veteran, I thank you for your service to our country, and I sincerely hope these meditations will bring you some encouragement.

G. M. McNally,
Panama City, Florida.
May 2025.

"Freedom is the oxygen of the soul."
Moshe Dayan

I

Who's The GOAT?

"Abram believed the Lord,
and He credited it to him as righteousness."
Genesis 15:6 (NIV).

"This is the only work God wants from you:
Believe in the one He has sent."
John 6:29 (NLT).

During the American Civil War, the Southern Confederacy did not award medals to its soldiers. Rather, the highest form of recognition given for outstanding service was to be mentioned in the official dispatches written by one's commanding officer. During the war, General Robert E. Lee mentioned cavalry officer Colonel John Singleton Mosby in his dispatches more than any other Confederate Soldier.

An unlikely hero, Mosby was a frail boy who was bullied in

his youth. He despised slavery yet felt it was his duty to fight for his "country," meaning Virginia. He enlisted in the Confederate Army as a private and, in time, became the leader of a cavalry unit known as "Mosby's Raiders." Daring and resourceful, Mosby became invaluable to the Confederacy and General Robert E. Lee. Lee frequently wrote about Mosby in his dispatches, leading some to refer to him as the Southern Confederacy's greatest soldier.

It is interesting to note that the person mentioned most often in the New Testament "dispatches" of Jesus Christ is Abraham. If you are surprised, it's probably because Abraham never did any of the things we usually associate with greatness. Spiritually speaking, he "never got his picture on a bubble gum card" (think of Lucy's beef with Schroeder in Peanuts). He was never a king or a writer of scripture like David. He was never a great leader of the masses like Moses. Abraham wasn't the great man of integrity that Daniel was. When he stood in fear before Pharaoh, he identified his wife as his sister (think of the 1960's song, *If You Wanna Be Happy for the Rest of Your Life*). And while Abraham rescued his nephew Lot from Chedorlaomer and the kings with him (Genesis 14:14-17), he was never a great military leader like Joshua.

The truth is that Abraham was great because of only one thing: *Abraham believed God.* And believing God is the greatest thing any person can do. Abraham is sometimes called '*our father in faith*'(Romans 4), and rightly so. Untold millions have followed his example. If you are a member of God's forever family, it is because you, like Abraham, your father in faith, simply believed the promise of God.

In recent years, the church seems to have drifted away from emphasizing what a person **believes** in favor of what a person **does**. The phrase "What Would Jesus Do?", often abbreviated to W.W.J.D., became particularly popular in the 1990's. The W.W.J.D. abbreviation stamped on wristbands became popular with Christian youth groups. The motto's focus was obedience, and the bracelets were a constant reminder to follow Jesus in a life of obedience. Living a life of obedience is a great and important step, but it isn't the first step. The first step is to BELIEVE what Jesus did for you on the cross. The next is to FOLLOW Him in a life of obedience.

When I first became a believer in the early 80's, it was common to hear a church leader ask, 'Is he (or she) a believer? Today, they are more likely to ask, "Is he (or she) a Christ follower?" Yes, it's a subtle shift, but not insignificant. The subtle message is, "We are focusing more on your lifestyle and not so much on what you believe."

Battle Plan

In his Gospel, John says that he wrote it for one purpose:

"*That you may believe that Jesus is the Christ, the Son of God, and that believing you may have life in His name.*"
John 20:31 (ESV).

In writing his Gospel, John uses the verb '*believe*' 98 times!

When sharing your faith with others, don't be afraid to use the word 'believe' (yes, even all by itself). John sure wasn't! Believing God is the greatest thing any person can do, and it's the only path to everlasting life.

> *"For God so loved the world that He gave His only begotten Son, that whoever believes in Him should not perish but have everlasting life."*
> John 3:16 (NKJV).

So shall your descendants be…
Craiyon.com

2

FULL ACCEPTANCE

"Therefore, the promise comes by faith so that it may be by grace and may be guaranteed to all Abraham's offspring."
Romans 4:16 (NIV).

During the Second World War, the U.S. Army created the "Individual Replacement System." When a unit suffered casualties, instead of recalling the entire unit for resupply of men, materials, and training, individual soldiers would be brought in to fill the gaps. These replacements were often just out of training and without any combat experience. The units they were assigned to were often comprised of men who had been together for years in training and combat.

These soldiers frequently struggled to integrate with their new unit and felt isolated and alone. Even the veteran soldiers who would normally be friendly were afraid to approach them. Earl McClung of Easy Company, Band of Brothers fame, said it this way:

> "I think maybe they [replacements] were trying to impress
> the older guys; people like me or Shifty or...
> I don't know why, but I got right there to where I didn't
> wanna be friendly with replacements coming in because,
> God, I just didn't like seeing 'em get killed.
> It just tore me up."

The Individual Replacement System may have solved the manpower issue in the short run, but it created some big problems for the replacements themselves in the long run. Most tried to earn acceptance by their performance, and combined with their lack of combat experience, the results were often deadly.

Just as soldiers fighting in a physical war need acceptance by their unit, soldiers fighting in a spiritual war need to know that they are fully accepted by God. The great reformers Martin Luther and John Calvin had their differences, but "full acceptance" is one thing they absolutely agreed on. Both men believed and taught that assurance of salvation (full acceptance) is an essential part of saving faith. So, when Jesus says, *"He who believes in Me has eternal life"* (John 6:47), I know that if I believe in Jesus, I have eternal life. I'm fully accepted. If I'm unsure I have eternal life, then I have not believed Jesus' words.

Fellow soldiers, we have the promise of our Commander in Chief, Jesus Christ, that we are fully accepted by Him through faith alone. He doesn't want us to doubt our acceptance in His forever family. The enemy will try to get you to 'confirm' your acceptance by looking to yourself and your performance or behavior. Don't do it! The results can be deadly! The truth is, none of us performs well enough. None of us behaves well enough. Don't look to yourself. Look to Jesus!

Battle Plan

When you go into battle, *take the helmet of salvation* with you (Ephesians 6:17). Don't let the enemy mess with your head!
Always remember:
You have been **fully accepted** by grace apart from all works.

"For it is by grace you have been saved through faith, and this is not from yourselves; it is the gift of God, not by works, so that no one can boast."
Ephesians 2:8-9 (NIV).

GARY MCNALLY

Brothers in Arms

3

U.S. GRANT

"A man's gift will make room for him."
Proverbs 18:16

When Confederate Guerrillas attacked Fort Sumter on April 14, 1861, Hiram Ulysses Grant was living in Galena, a small town on the Mississippi River in Northwest Illinois. After graduating from the U.S. Military Academy at West Point in 1843, he served with distinction as a Lieutenant in the U.S. Army during the Mexican-American War. In 1854, while serving in California, he resigned his commission and returned to his family in Missouri.

Over the next seven years, Grant worked hard to provide for his family. He tried his hand at farming and managed his father-in-law's farm for a time. That was not sufficiently lucrative, so he tried selling real estate. Then, for a time, he took a job as a debt collector, and, at one point, he sold firewood in the streets of St Louis to provide for his family.

During this time, Grant likely cemented his reputation as having little or no business sense. Some have noted that this was evident when he purchased a slave, William Jones, from his father-in-law and then, shortly after, freed him. Though he desperately needed money, Grant didn't require William to earn his freedom, nor did he try to sell William at auction. He just set him free.

By 1859, Grant was financially desperate. His father had a tannery business in Galena, Illinois, and had been trying for some time to get Ulysses to move to Illinois. His father finally persuaded him, and in 1860, Grant moved his family 300 miles north, where he assumed a job as a clerk in his father's tannery business.

In his widely acclaimed series *"The Civil War,"* Ken Burns introduces Grant by describing him as "A lackluster clerk from Galena, IL. A failure in everything except marriage and war…" It may have suited Burns's purposes to portray Grant that way, but no man is without God-given gifts and talents. Just a few of Grant's abilities included,

A Gifted Horseman - Horses were Grant's lifelong passion. By the age of five, he was riding on horseback in a standing position. He also perfected the ability to lift one leg and balance himself on the other. Grant's classmates at West Point said that watching Grant ride a horse was "better than going to the circus."

Loyalty—Grant was fiercely loyal to friends and family.

Having known and served with R. E. Lee before the war, it was Grant who lobbied President Andrew Johnson to drop charges of treason against Lee after the war. Johnson initially refused, but Grant was unmoved and threatened to resign. Sensing that he needed Grant in his corner after the war, Johnson eventually gave in.

Courage - Civil War Historian Shelby Foote said that Grant had "Four o'clock in the morning courage." Foote explained, "...the courage it takes to stay calm when you are woken up at 4:00 am and told your left flank has just been turned." Grant's courage in battle was almost legendary. His own soldiers liked to say, "Ulysses don't scare worth a damn."

Battle Plan

Have you ever felt like a failure? Have you ever thought that you have little or nothing to offer in the battle of the Christian life? Think again. God has gifted you. Use what He has given you with renewed strength today. Use it until the Lord redeploys you, or the battle is over. US Grant became the 18th President of the United States. His gifts made room for him. Yours will make room for you.

"God has given each of you a gift from His great variety of spiritual gifts. Use them well to serve one another."
1 Peter 4:10 (NLT).

GARY MCNALLY

*Ulysses S. Grant at his headquarters
in Cold Harbor, Virginia, June 1864.*

4

THE WALKING DEAD

"I have been crucified with Christ; it is no longer I who live,
but Christ lives in me; and the life which I now live in the flesh
I live by faith in the Son of God,
Who loved me and gave Himself for me."
Galatians 2:20 (NKJV).

In the HBO miniseries *Band of Brothers*, paratrooper Albert
Blithe recounts his struggle with paralyzing fear on the
Normandy battlefield to Lieutenant Ronald Speirs. Speirs
gives Blithe the essential key to successful soldiering. He must
reckon himself "already dead."

It isn't a difficult concept to understand, but it can be
difficult to implement and sustain. Speirs was an extremely
effective soldier who seemed to have practiced what he
preached. Later, in a battle for the small town of Foy, Speirs
would take a gamble, illustrating his "already dead" mindset.

On January 13, 1945, Lt. Speirs was ordered to assume command of a failing assault on a German position in the small Belgian town of Foy. Easy Company of the 506th Parachute Infantry Regiment of the 101st Airborne Division was stalled in their offensive when Spiers took over. One segment of the Easy Company attack had gone on a flanking move around some farm buildings on the edge of the village to try to get behind the Germans. Speirs wanted to recall the men from the flanking movement, but had no radio communication with them.

As Sargent Carwood Lipton would later testify, Speirs ran straight through the village, past enemy soldiers, and found his men on the other side. Having given them new orders, he turned around and ran back through the village again, right past a German artillery battery. Some Germans seemed so busy supplying the artillery piece that they hardly noticed Speirs. Others stood in shock as he ran right past them, first on his way in and then on his way back out.

Lieutenant Speirs was not a foolish man. He looked at the situation and realized he had to recall his men. The Germans would never expect an enemy soldier to run right past them (and certainly not twice), and there were obstacles that Speirs could weave in and out of, which would provide a few seconds of cover as he ran. Speirs reckoned that was all he would need. He assessed the situation and took a calculated risk. If it failed, oh well, he was already dead anyway.

I became a Christian soldier at the age of 26 in March of 1980. At that time, I understood and believed that Christ's death on the cross had done everything that God required for me to be justified in His sight and to spend eternity with Him.

I didn't become an effective Christian Soldier, however, until my baptism four years later at the age of 30. I realized I was tired of being ineffective and decided I needed to become a full-time soldier of Christ or a full-time Epicurean.

> *"Let us eat and drink, for tomorrow we die!"*
> 1 Corinthians 15:32 (NKJV).

The latter didn't seem to be a viable option for me at that time. I fully understood that by being baptized, I would be acknowledging that I had "*died with Christ*" and that I needed to become a walking, talking "dead man" in the Lord's army. I followed through and was baptized as the Bible commands.

I wish I could say I have always sustained that "already dead" status, but that wouldn't be true. However, the overall trajectory has been upward, and my only regret is that I waited for four years.

Battle Plan

Have you believed in Jesus for the free gift of eternal life? If so, it's time to step up! It's time to accept your position as having died with Christ and to proclaim it publicly through baptism. It's the only real hope you have on the battlefield of life. What are you waiting for?

5

Traveling Alone

"Two are better than one because they have a good reward for
their labor. For if they fall, one will lift up his companion.
But woe to him who is alone when he falls."
Ecclesiastes 4:9-10 (NKJV).

On March 19, 1943, the U.S. Submarine *Kingfish* was on her 3rd war patrol near Formosa (present-day Taiwan). Her skipper was Lt. Cdr. Vernon "Rebel" Lowrance, a 1930 graduate of the U.S. Naval Academy. *Kingfish* intercepted a large Japanese troop transport, *Takachiho Maru*, which was taking reinforcements to the Philippine Islands. Commander Lowrance was surprised that the ship was traveling alone without a destroyer escort. Lowrance fired four torpedoes, three of which hit the ship. One was a dud, but two exploded and mortally wounded the transport. The ship sank by the stern just 10 minutes after being hit, and approximately 850 Japanese soldiers and sailors went down with her.

Just a few days later, while traveling on the surface at 0300, *Kingfish* encountered a single Japanese Destroyer sailing alone. Was this the missing escort trying to rendezvous with the *Takachiho Maru*? The destroyer caught *Kingfish* in its spotlight and charged. The submarine dove and tried to evade the destroyer but was immediately subjected to a fierce, well-executed depth charge attack. The destroyer dropped forty depth charges over the next eight hours with unusual accuracy.

At one point in the attack, two depth charge explosions caused significant flooding, while another charge exploded so close to the sub that it buckled the outer hull. The attack was so fierce that Commander Lowrance promised God that if they survived, he and his entire crew would attend church together to thank Him for saving them.

The crew worked together to make emergency repairs, *and Kingfish* and her crew survived and returned safely to Pearl Harbor on April 9, 1943. Lowrance and his crew went to church together and thanked God for their survival.

The fact is, Christian soldiers also need each other. We're in a war. Traveling alone is almost always a bad idea. Men hate to admit they need help. At least I do. My wife finds my unwillingness to ask for help to be one of my greatest flaws. My reply usually goes something like this, "It's not that I don't want help. It's just that I hate to bother a friend. They are busy just like us!" So, this week, when I needed a couple of zip ties to attach a flag to a pole, I decided to ask my new neighbor for help. He had the ties and was only too happy to assist, and as a result, we got to know each other better. It wasn't as painful as I expected!

Battle Plan

Brother in arms, the battle is long and hard, and we need each other.

- Do you have a neighbor you could borrow from instead of running to the store and buying it?
- Are you regularly attending a Bible-believing church? Have you joined a small group?

Don't be afraid to ask for help. Don't make the mistake of traveling alone. It's not as much fun, and it can be very dangerous!

Let us think of ways to motivate one another to acts of love and good works. And let us not neglect our meeting together, as some people do, but encourage one another, especially now that the day of his return is drawing near.
Hebrews 10:24–25. (NLT).

USS Kingfish; September 1944.
(U.S. Navy Bureau of Ships Photograph 19-N-72408, National Archives and Records Administration, Still Pictures Division, College Park, Md.)

6

The Seal Ethos

"Therefore, do not cast away your confidence,
which has great reward."
Hebrews 10:35 (NKJV)

In June of 2005, Navy SEAL Lieutenant Michael Murphy and three fellow SEALs were deployed in the Hindu Kush Mountain range in Afghanistan. Their mission was to locate an insurgent leader working with the Taliban. In the process, they encountered three goat tenders who later betrayed their presence to the Taliban.

Murphy and his men were then pursued by a group of Taliban fighters in platoon strength, resulting in a huge firefight. As the fight developed, all four SEALs were wounded, and Murphy repeatedly called for help, but the mountainous terrain blocked their radio signal.

Murphy began leading his men toward higher ground in the hope of securing assistance, all the while under fire from the Taliban fighters who were in hot pursuit. Murphy was finally successful in making radio contact, but he was shot in the back while making the call and dropped the radio. Despite his injury, he was able to pick it up, complete the call, and return fire on the enemy. Out in the open for radio communication and suffering multiple gunshot wounds, Murphy made his way back to cover with his three SEAL comrades.

Murphy's call for help resulted in a Chinook helicopter being dispatched with eight seals and eight Army special forces personnel to recover the men. However, tragedy struck when the aircraft was hit by an enemy RPG, resulting in a crash that claimed the lives of everyone aboard. Murphy and his team fought for several hours, neutralizing 20-30 of the enemy fighters. Soon, however, only one member, Marcus Luttrell, was still alive. Luttrell was rendered unconscious by another RPG, but when he awoke, he was able to evade the remaining Taliban fighters. Luttrell was the only survivor. Badly wounded, he managed to walk and crawl seven miles to avoid capture. He was given shelter and cared for by a friendly Afghan tribe, who alerted the Americans of his presence, and American forces finally rescued him six days after the gun battle.

Luttrell's account was portrayed in the movie *Lone Survivor*. He demonstrated true SEAL heroism and was ultimately awarded the Navy Cross and Purple Heart for his actions.

In part, the Navy SEAL ethos says,

"I will never quit. I persevere and thrive on adversity. My nation expects me to be physically harder and mentally stronger than my enemies.
If knocked down, I will get back up every time.
I will draw on every remaining ounce of strength to protect my teammates and to accomplish our mission."

Lt. Michael Murphy. Navy.mil

Lieutenant Michael Murphy and his team truly reflect that ethos: "I will never quit." In October 2007, Michael Murphy was posthumously awarded the Medal of Honor for his leadership and selfless courage.

As with their SEAL counterparts, it is the duty of Christian Soldiers to never quit. In the Bible, the book of Hebrews was written specifically to challenge Christian soldiers to never stop fighting. The book is filled with encouragement to *press on to maturity.* Soldiers need heroes like Lt. Murphy to encourage and inspire them in earthly warfare. Soldiers engaged in spiritual warfare need heroes, too.

Hebrews chapter 11 gives a long list of heroes. Who is your favorite hero, and why? They all had one thing in common: Despite seemingly impossible challenges, they refused to quit and displayed incredible trust in their heavenly Commander. They are the "SEALs" of the Lord's army.

Battle Plan

Hey, soldier, are you thinking about quitting? Don't even go there. Think you aren't strong enough or courageous enough? That can be a good thing (see 2 Corinthians 12:10). Remember, scripture says those who stick it out can gain *"an even better resurrection"* at the end of their deployment (Hebrews 11:35; see also 2 Peter 1:11). Hang tough and keep looking up!

*"...Let us run with endurance the race that is set before us,
looking unto Jesus, the Author and Finisher of our faith,
Who for the joy that was set before Him
endured the cross..."*
Hebrews 12:1-2 (NKJV).

33

7

Benedict Arnold

Pride goes before destruction,
and a haughty spirit before a fall.
Proverbs 16:18 (NKJV).

George Washington called him his "fighting general." He had been a successful businessman and a staunch American Patriot. Yet, tragically, he is only remembered as a traitor. Born and raised in Connecticut, Benedict Arnold was among the first to champion American independence. He was a brilliant tactician and courageous in battle.

- In May 1775, Arnold seized and held Fort Ticonderoga.
- In December of that year, at George Washington's request, Arnold led an army against the British in Quebec City. The hope was to drive the British out of Canada and convince the citizens of Quebec to join the

patriot cause. While the effort failed, Arnold led well and fought bravely.

- In October 1776, he fought a delaying action against the British on Lake Champlain that greatly helped the patriot cause.
- Perhaps Arnold's greatest victory was at Saratoga in October 1777. He led an attack on Breymann's Redoubt that was decisive in winning the battle for the Americans.

While Arnold's leadership on the battlefield at Saratoga brought the victory, the credit at the time was wrongly given to General Horatio Gates, the overall commander of the Continental forces. Some even labeled Gates "the hero of Saratoga."

Arnold felt slighted. He felt that his sacrifice, efforts, and leadership in the patriot cause were unappreciated. He had been severely wounded in the leg during the fight at Quebec City and was wounded again at Saratoga in the same leg. The wounds left him partially crippled for the rest of his life, yet he saw little in the way of reward.

Adding insult to physical injury, in 1777, the Continental Congress promoted five men to Major General, and Arnold, who deserved the promotion, was passed over. It is unclear why, but again, Arnold felt insulted and resentful. He appealed to George Washington, who agreed that he should have been promoted. Washington urged Arnold not to quit the cause regardless of the slight.

He was finally promoted to Major General, but without the seniority that would place him over those promoted before him. Arnold was again slighted. It took two more years and some other difficult circumstances for the emotional wounds to fully fester, but in September of 1780, Arnold met with British Major John Andre and agreed to turn over the West Point, NY garrison to the British. In return, he was to receive a large cash sum and a position in the British Army. Arnold had officially earned the label of "traitor."

Treason seems to be the greatest sin for a soldier, and pride seems to be the ultimate character flaw. A soldier may be a gifted leader with great courage and good intentions, but all these qualities can be destroyed by pride and self-love. If you are a Christian soldier, you aren't in it for yourself. You're in it for the One who loved you and gave Himself for you. Like Him, you are called to humble yourself and make yourself of "*no reputation*"(Philippians 2:7).

In May 1995, Chuck Swindoll spoke privately to his first graduating class as President of Dallas Seminary. He took the graduates aside and said (paraphrased):

"God isn't looking for people
who want to make a name for themselves.
He isn't looking for people willing to be famous for Him.
There is no shortage there.
He is looking for people who are willing
to be anonymous for Him."

Battle Plan

The Bible teaches that the Lord's servant soldier, who is anonymous here on earth, will be publicly recognized and richly rewarded in glory. Do you believe that? Are you willing to forego praise and recognition in this present world? You can have it here (Matthew 6:2), or you can have it hereafter. It's your call.

And behold, I am coming quickly, and My reward is with Me, to give to every one according to his work.
Revelation 22:12 (NKJV).

The Saratoga Boot Monument honors Benedict Arnold's leadership in winning the battle of Saratoga, but does not mention his name because he later betrayed his country.

8

The Memphis Belle

*"Today, you are on the verge of battle with your enemies. Do
not let your heart faint, do not be afraid,
and do not tremble or be terrified because of them;
for the Lord your God is He who goes with you,
to fight for you against your enemies, to save you.'"*
Deuteronomy 20:3-4 (NKJV).

The Memphis Belle was a U.S. Army Air Forces B-17
heavy bomber in the 91st Bombardment Group during WW2.
The crew flew their first combat mission on November 7, 1942,
and their 25th and final mission on May 19, 1943. They were one
of the first crews to complete 25 combat missions over Nazi-
occupied Europe. Having reached this milestone, the
Memphis Belle and her crew flew back to the United States on
June 8, 1943.

In the 1990 Hollywood film *Memphis Belle*, one of the crew members read aloud a portion of a poem by W. B. Yeats during a delay in taking off for a bombing mission;

> I know that I shall meet my fate.
> Somewhere among the clouds above.
> Those that I fight, I do not hate
> Those that I guard, I do not love;
>
> Nor law nor duty bade me fight,
> Nor public man, nor cheering crowds,
> A lonely impulse of delight
> Drove to this tumult in the clouds;
>
> I balanced all, brought all to mind,
> The years to come seemed waste of breath,
> A waste of breath, the years behind
> In balance with this life, this death.

His crewmates, sitting all around him, fell silent. You could see and feel the impact of the words.

Most men confess that the experience of war is the most terrible of their lives. Others will admit to the horror of war and yet seem to be able to rise above it all and focus on the camaraderie and ultimate benefit of the conflict, especially if they are on the winning side. One thing seems beyond dispute. *The experience of war defines all those who participate.* For better or worse, nothing impacts a soldier's life more than the demands and challenges of war.

Soldier, you are in a war. For better or worse, it will define you. Maybe you are here because you feel you were "drafted." Or perhaps you found Christianity interesting and enlisted.

Whatever the reason, you're here, and it will be best for you if you fight and fight well. At the end of his life, the Apostle Paul, possibly the greatest soldier of all, said, *"I have fought the good fight... I have kept the faith"* (2 Timothy 4:7, NIV). I pray you and I can say the same when our fight is over.

Battle Plan

How's your fight going? Your eternal **destination** is already secure because Christ has finished His fight on your behalf. However, your eternal **reward** will be determined by how well you fight from now till your war is over. Is there any baggage slowing you down? If so, today is probably a good day to get rid of it.

Look to yourselves that we do not lose those things we worked for, but that we may receive a full reward.
2 John 8 (NKJV).

"Looking back on the war, despite the really bad times, it was certainly the most exciting experience of my life...
As I see it, at that young age, we hit the climax.
Everything after that is anticlimactic."
Richard Prendergast
WW2 combat veteran, as quoted in *The Good War*.

The Memphis Belle and crew after their 25th mission.
(U.S. Air Force photo).

9

Blessed are the Light-Hearted

"He who is of a merry heart has a continual feast."
Proverbs 15:15b (NKJV).

It is hard to imagine how anyone gets through the battle of life without humor. The Bible is replete with humor. Sometimes it is sarcastic, sometimes it's ironic, and sometimes it's absurd. Some biblical humor is obvious. Some is implied. And yes, some can even be imagined. After all, humor is an art form!

There are no specific references in the gospels to Jesus and His disciples joking with each other, but does anyone doubt that 13 men traveling and living together for more than two years occasionally joked with each other? I can easily imagine Peter, on a dare from James and John, approaching Jesus and saying, "Rabbi, pull my finger." ** Of course, they joked with each other!

Sarcastic humor is evident in 1 Kings 18 when Elijah faced off against the prophets of Baal on Mt. Carmel. The Baal prophets could not get their god to answer despite hours of pleading. Elijah responded by telling them to *"Shout louder! Perhaps he is deep in thought, or busy, or traveling"* (1 Kings 18:27). Absurd humor was seen when God spoke to Balaam through his donkey in Numbers 22.

Humor is critical for soldiers. It is no secret that some of the most therapeutic humor comes from wartime. After a bloody Civil War battle, a newspaper writer remarked that "off-hand" jokes were in good supply at the surgeon's tent. Another commented that suing for financial support from the government would be futile for double-leg amputees, as the courts would say they "didn't have a leg to stand on."

In his book "War Fish," George Grider tells the story of an "elderly" submariner who was making his first war patrol on the USS Wahoo during WW2. The Wahoo had just torpedoed a Japanese ship off Honshu and was making her getaway while submerged. The man was talking to some shipmates when a Japanese plane dropped depth charges near the sub. When one exploded, the man stopped speaking and looked up with eyes wide and mouth open. His upper denture detached and landed on the lower one as he stood there. Grider writes,

"The sight of this startled submariner standing there with his mouth open and his teeth shut was more than anyone in the torpedo room could stand. Depth charges or not, every man present doubled up and howled with glee."

On Guadalcanal in 1943, a Marine Corps advance had been pinned down by a Japanese machine gun nest. Several marines were lying low in a huge crater created by an artillery shell. Captain Henry P. Crowe burst in on them and said,

"G*dd*m*t, you'll never get a Purple Heart hiding in a foxhole. Follow me!"

They burst out of the hole and followed Captain Crowe, and I have to believe most of them had a smile on their face!
Capt. Henry P. "Jim" Crowe, USMC, Guadalcanal, 13 Jan. 1943

Battle Plan

Humor is essential for Christian soldiers. Had a good laugh lately? Don't listen to the naysayers who think you shouldn't joke about the really painful things that happen in the struggle of life. To be sure, love and discernment must dictate time and place, but almost nothing is too sacred to forbid a chuckle.

"If I did not laugh, I should die."
Abraham Lincoln

"See me safe up,
for my coming down, I can shift for myself."
Sir Thomas More
(on needing help ascending the stairs to his execution).

"A cheerful heart is good medicine,
but a crushed spirit dries up the bones."
Proverbs 17:22 (NIV).

** Of course, Jesus didn't fall for it. He just smiled, shook his head, and rolled his eyes.

IO

Soldiers In Hiding

*"Joseph of Arimathea... was a disciple of Jesus,
but secretly because he feared the Jewish leaders."*
John 19:38 (NIV).

Georg Gaertner was a member of Erwin Rommel's "Afrika
Korps" when he was captured near Tunis in 1943. Like many
thousands of other German POWs, he was then shipped to the
U.S. for internment. There were some 500 POW facilities in
the U.S. by the end of WW2, and Gaertner was held at Camp
Deming, New Mexico.

During his two years at Camp Deming, Gaertner became
fluent in English. Shortly after the war ended in 1945, he
escaped from the camp. Gaertner managed to dig undetected
under two fence barriers and then jumped a westbound train
that passed nearby.

Over the next 40 years, Gaertner lived in several U.S.

States. He first went by the name Peter Petersen, then later Dennis Whiles. He managed to elude authorities while working as a lumberjack, ski instructor, tennis pro, artist, and contractor. Gaertner mastered the art of blending in. He held many jobs and traveled to many places. He even got married in 1964, yet he always managed to hide his true identity.

Finally, in 1984, his wife became frustrated with the oddities and inconsistencies he had accumulated over the years. She threatened to leave him if he didn't tell her the truth. He finally told her the truth. The next year, he told the world.

Georg Gaertner isn't the first soldier who wanted to hide his identity. In my experience, Christian soldiers sometimes do it too. The reasons are many, but they usually boil down to the fear of someone or something.

When I first became a believer in my late 20's, I hesitated to say so. I had several reasons, all of which were rooted in either fear or pride. My pride didn't allow me to admit to my new Baptist friends that they were right and that the theological tradition I grew up in was wrong. I was also afraid I wouldn't be able to keep all the 'rules' that those same friends seemed to live by. I even put off being baptized for several years for fear of 'going public,' I mean, what if I can't do this? It's a lot more convenient to just fly under the radar. That way, when I mess up, hopefully, no one will notice!

Battle Plan

Fellow soldier, don't let pride and/or fear paralyze you. It's a terrible way to live! If you have been in the Lord's Army for a time but are currently "AWOL," get back to your unit (or find a new one) and get back in the fight! If you are new to the Lord's army, then don't be afraid to say so. Get baptized and tell the world who you really are. You will never regret it!

"Has the LORD redeemed you? Then speak out!"
Psalm 107:2 (NLT).

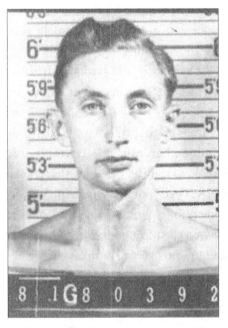

German P.O.W. Georg Gaertner, FBI.

II

Faulty Weapons

"The weapons we fight with are not the weapons of the world. On the contrary, they have divine power to demolish strongholds."
2 Corinthians 10:4 (NIV).

In November 1942, the U.S. Submarine Seawolf, under Lieutenant Commander Fred Warder, discovered the Japanese transport ship Sagami Maru at anchor in Davao Gulf, Philippines. As Warder sized up the vessel through his periscope, his mind drifted back to the previous April when the Seawolf had attacked three different Japanese Cruisers. All three attacks failed to damage, much less sink, the enemy ships. After the third attack, the Seawolf endured a brutal depth charge attack that lasted nearly two days and from which she only barely escaped. Warder felt certain that the problem was faulty torpedoes.

Now, with the Sagami Maru in sight, Commander Warder was determined to prove his point. He approached the enemy ship at close range and fired four successive torpedoes.

- The first passed under the ship and exploded on the beach beyond. The magnetic exploder failed to detonate.
- The second torpedo detonated just before it got to the enemy ship, causing violent rocking but no damage.
- The third torpedo passed directly under again and failed to explode, evidently lodging in the mud near the beach.
- A fourth torpedo behaved exactly like the third.

Warder and his crew had meticulously documented every setting and calculation of each torpedo firing sequence and also taken pictures through the periscope. He finally had hard evidence that the weapons were faulty.

Captain Edward L. Beach, himself a WW2 submariner, pointed out that torpedo failure rates for U.S. Pacific Subs were approximately 85% in the first year of the Pacific War with Japan. These submariners risked their lives in possibly the most dangerous and demanding field of battle only to have their weapons fail them. The devastating effect on morale can only be imagined.

Captain Beach says in his book *Submarine:*

"Our submarines were being sent to war with defective
weapons. They had not one but two enemies...
No one, even now, dares hazard a guess as to how many
submarines sleep the everlasting sleep
because of this insidious foe."[1]

In 2 Corinthians 10, the apostle Paul reminds us that
Christian soldiers have superior weapons with which to fight.
They are superior because they have *divine power.* Our
Commander doesn't make faulty weapons. If I am not
effective in the battle of the Christian life, the fault lies with
me, not my weapons.

Are you using your weapons and using them properly?

Battle Plan

Yesterday I went shopping at Sam's Club. A guy walked
by with what looked like a beehive on top of his head. He had
lots of other body 'decorations,' not the least of which was a
large nose ring. My first thought was, 'Look at this
knucklehead!'

---

[1] Edward L. Beach, *Submarine,* 20

My second thought was, "No, you're the knucklehead. You have no idea what strongholds, struggles, or pain this guy may be dealing with. Pray for him!" So, I did.

One of our weapons is prayer. It will never fail! Use it. Use it properly and use it often.

Faulty Mark 14 Torpedo, Pearl Harbor, Hawaii.
https://pearl-harbor.info/the-mark-14-torpedo-problem-child-of-the-us-navy/

12

War Bonds

"He who has begun a good work in you
will complete it until the day of Jesus Christ."
Philippians 1:6 (NKJV).

War is not only destructive, it's also very expensive. Armies are made up of soldiers, and soldiers require a steady supply of resources. During WW2, all the Allied and Axis nations sold "war bonds" to finance their war efforts. Sensing that the U.S. would eventually become involved in the war in Europe, the U.S. government began selling "Defense Bonds" in 1939. The name was quickly changed to "War Bonds" after the Japanese attack on Pearl Harbor.

A bond would usually be purchased at around two-thirds of its face value, so you could buy a $100 bond for around $65, and it would usually mature in 10 years. War bonds are typically non-transferable, so they are only payable to the owner or co-owner of the bond.

The U.S. Government raised approximately 180 billion dollars during the war by selling war bonds. In the United

States, Hollywood stars like Bob Hope, Bing Crosby, and Dorothy Lamour traveled across the country, showcasing their talents in performances to promote bond sales.

Most people didn't buy war bonds because it was the most profitable way to invest their money. Rather, they did so out of a sense of patriotic duty. They were proud of their country and wanted to see it survive and prosper. Citizens could effectively become partners in the war effort by purchasing these bonds.

War bonds can be a risky investment, especially if your side doesn't win. After WW2, Japanese war bonds were essentially worthless for years because of hyperinflation and overall economic turmoil.

The Philippian Church has been called "Paul's favorite church," and for good reason. They had repeatedly sent financial aid and supplies to support Paul as he spread the Gospel throughout the Roman Empire. Paul said he "*thanked the Lord for them every time he thought of them.*" Why? Because of their "*fellowship* [sharing, partnership] *in the gospel.*" Paul is referring specifically to the financial support of the Philippians. He says their support is a "*good work*" and that the Lord Himself "*will complete it until the day of Jesus Christ.*" Philippians 1:5-6 (NKJV).

The Philippians had taken out a "war bond" on Paul's behalf, which was already accruing interest! Paul stated that even though he was in prison, his captors, the *Praetorian Guard* (Philippians 1:13), were hearing the Gospel, which was now being preached boldly throughout Rome. As Paul continued to win converts, those converts would win more converts, and so on and so on, "*until the day of Jesus Christ.*"

That is compounding interest at its best!

Battle Plan

Fellow soldiers, we know who wins in the end, so investing in Christian "war bonds" is kind of a no-brainer. It's almost like legalized insider trading! How is your heavenly 401K doing? It's an investment opportunity that will pay eternal dividends, and yes, you *can* take it with you!

> *"Lay up for yourselves treasures in heaven,*
> *where neither moth nor rust destroys*
> *and where thieves do not break in and steal."*
> Matthew 6:20 (NKJV).

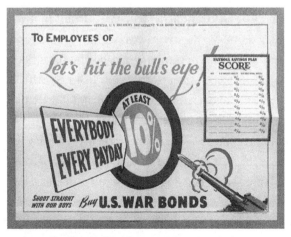

U.S. War Bonds, Northwestern University Libraries.

13

Sam and Pete

"A friend loves at all times,
and a brother is born for adversity."
Proverbs 17:17 (NKJV).

When Ulysses Grant arrived at West Point in 1839 for his "Plebe" year, James Longstreet was beginning his second year at the Academy. The two men could hardly have been more different. Longstreet was a Southerner from South Carolina and Georgia. Grant was a northern boy from Ohio. Longstreet was 6'-2", while Grant was only 5'-8". The one thing the two men seemed to share was an uncommon love of horses.

Ulysses "Sam" Grant and James "Pete" Longstreet. Two disparate men who became friends and, despite being on opposite sides in the bloodiest war in American history, were able to maintain a friendship that lasted a lifetime. After graduating from West Point, both men were assigned to

Jefferson Barracks, Missouri. Fred Dent, a fellow West Point Graduate and Longstreet's cousin, was posted there with them.

Dent's family home was nearby, and while visiting Dent's family, Grant met his sister, Julia. Sometime later, Ulysses and Julia would marry, with Longstreet and his new bride in attendance. The two men served together in the Mexican-American War but were then separated for years by their career paths. Then, in 1861, the country was engulfed in the flames of the Civil War.

What is it that causes some friendships to endure and others to fade? Though the Civil War would severely test their friendship, it would not end it. The next time the two men met would be immediately following Lee's surrender to Grant at Appomattox Court House in April of 1865.

One of the times the two men had enjoyed over the years was playing an old British card game called Brag. After the surrender, Grant evidently noticed Longstreet standing with a group of Confederate officers. Grant immediately walked over to Longstreet, grabbed his hand, and said, "Pete, let's have another game of Brag to recall the pleasant days." Longstreet was nearly overcome with emotion and would later write, "Great God! I thought to myself, how my heart swells out to such a magnanimous touch of humanity. Why do men fight who were born to be brothers?"

Why indeed.

Battle Plan

Is there an old friend you have fallen out with or have just been out of touch with? Might it be good to pray for that friend and then follow up by reaching out somehow? There is no telling what the Lord might do!

"Love prospers when a fault is forgiven,
but dwelling on it separates close friends."
Proverbs 17:9 (NLT).

A faithful friend is a sturdy shelter; he who finds one finds a treasure. A faithful friend is beyond price.
No sum can balance his worth.
Sirach (Ecclesiasticus)

Ulysses Grant and James Longstreet.

14

Precious Death

"Precious in the sight of the LORD
is the death of His saints."
Psalm 116:15 (NKJV).

In 1755, Nathan Hale was born into a devout Christian family in Connecticut. Throughout his short life, he was described as kind, gentle, handsome, and athletic. Hale was a committed Christian and was known for his Scripture memory. A graduate of Yale and a teacher by trade, he left his profession to become a patriot soldier.

Hale was known for caring for and praying with his men when they were sick or troubled. In 1775, morale was an issue in the fledgling Continental Army, and Hale would share his pay with his men who were in need. By late summer of 1776, the British had invaded Long Island, and the Continental Army under George Washington was deployed on Manhattan

Island. Washington desperately needed information on the size, strength, and location of British forces. The only way to get trustworthy information was to send someone (a spy) from the Continental Army.

Against the advice of trusted friends, Captain Hale volunteered. In early September 1776, he slipped across the East River onto Long Island in civilian clothes, disguised appropriately as a school teacher looking for work. It has never been clear how Hale was discovered or who, if anyone, might have betrayed him, but on September 21, he was stopped and found to have incriminating evidence of spying on his person. Hale quickly confessed to the British his true identity and was immediately sentenced to death by hanging. That sentence was carried out the very next day. 21-year-old Captain Nathan Hale was hanged on September 22, 1776.

Many people know Nathan Hale's famous last words, "I regret that I have but one life to lose for my country." By all reports, those were his last words, but they were not his only words. British Lieutenant Robert McKensie was present at the hanging. He wrote of being impressed with Hale's "great composure and resolution." He recorded Hale advising the crowd on hand to "be at all times prepared to meet death in whatever shape it might appear."

Why are some soldiers, even Christian soldiers, so afraid of death? The Bible tells us that Jesus died to *free those who, all their lives, were held in slavery by their fear of death* (Hebrews 2:15, NIV). Nearly everything we see and hear from the world around us tells us that death is the end of everything and the grave is forever. Not true! Death is the gateway to eternity! Jesus said,

> *"I am the resurrection and the life. He who believes in Me, though he may die, he shall live."*
> John 11:25 (NKJV)

Do you believe that, fellow soldier?

Battle Plan

If you cannot, at this moment, accept the prospect of death without fear, then accept by faith that you need not fear it. Think of Paul's words. Think of Jesus' words. Think of the words of 21-year-old Nathan Hale.

> *"For, to me, to live is Christ, and to die is gain."*
> Philippians 1:21 (NIV).

> "Someday, you will read in the papers that D. L. Moody, of East Northfield, is dead. Don't you believe a word of it! At that moment, I shall be more alive than I am now."
> Dwight. L. Moody

Statue of Nathan Hale in Washington, D.C.

15

USS WAHOO

(Counting The Cost)

*"What king, going to make war against another king,
does not sit down first and consider whether he is able with
ten thousand to meet him,
who comes against him with twenty thousand?"*
Luke 14:31 (NKJV).

The most successful U.S. Submarine in WW2 was the
USS Tang. She sank 33 ships for a total tonnage of 116,454.
But, while Tang was the most successful sub, she was not
necessarily the best known. The USS Wahoo sank 27 ships
and was skippered by Lieutenant Commander Dudley "Mush"
Morton. Born and raised in the South, Morton had been a
gifted athlete at the U.S. Naval Academy, where he acquired
the nickname "Mush Mouth" because of his notable southern
drawl.

As skipper of Wahoo, Morton gained a reputation for

daring. His exploits quickly became both controversial and legendary. In early January 1943, on his first war patrol as skipper of Wahoo, Morton was ordered to "reconnoiter" the Japanese-held Wewak Harbor on the north coast of New Guinea. To most sub-commanders, reconnoiter meant to sit a safe distance outside the harbor and mark the comings and goings of enemy shipping. Morton had other ideas. He took Wahoo into the harbor.

Wewak Harbor was about seven miles long and shaped like a dog leg. Wahoo made its way into the harbor, reaching a spot where they could glimpse the upper section but found it empty. Continuing for several more miles, they reached the lower section and spotted a Japanese destroyer anchored there.

Most submarine commanders would not have attacked the destroyer inside the harbor because they were at least six miles from the open ocean and had less than 200 feet of water under them. Quite honestly, most sub-commanders would never have entered Wewak Harbor in the first place. But Mush Morton was not like most commanders. He said, "We'll take him by complete surprise. He won't be expecting an enemy submarine in here." George Grider was an officer on the Wahoo at the time and in his book *War Fish*, recalls thinking, "Nobody in his right mind would have expected us in here."

Moments later, the destroyer had gotten underway and was heading in Wahoo's direction, making the decision to attack even more questionable. Morton fired four torpedoes at the destroyer as it crossed Wahoo's bow. All missed astern. They had underestimated the destroyer's speed. Now very aware of Wahoo's presence, the destroyer was headed directly at them.

Wahoo had fired four of her six bow torpedoes, and there was no time to reload. Morton ordered a "down-the-throat" shot with torpedo #5 (firing at the destroyer's bow as it charged head-on). It missed. When the Japanese commander saw #6 heading right at him, he elected to try to turn away and was struck amidship. The destroyer literally broke in two. Morton had taken a very big gamble, and it paid off.

In January 1956, five young American missionaries were speared to death by the Auca Indians of eastern Ecuador, whom they had been trying to reach with the good news of the Gospel of Grace. The five men understood the risk. The Aucas had a reputation for ferocity and killing, yet despite this, they landed their plane in the remote area and personally contacted the Aucas with no weapons for protection. Their story was portrayed in the 2005 film "*End of the Spear.*"

How much risk is too much in the battle of the Christian life? Can you be too aggressive? How do you strike a balance between living by faith and just being foolhardy?

In September 1943, Wahoo departed Pearl Harbor for her fifth war patrol and second venture into the dangerous waters of the Sea of Japan. The Wahoo was not ordered to go; Commander Morton requested the assignment. During a Japanese depth charge attack in October 1943, Wahoo was lost with all 79 crew members. How much risk is too much? Your answer might not be the same as mine, and that's ok.

Battle Plan

Be sure you honestly assess your risk tolerance. In the parable of Luke 14 (above), there would be no shame in deciding not to go to war with another king when you are outnumbered 2 to 1. There might also be a scenario where you would go to war even when outnumbered that badly if there were other mitigating circumstances. The point is that taking on a life of discipleship should not be taken lightly. You should know what you are getting into and be honest about your own tolerance for hardship and risk. As Shakespeare said, "To thine own self be true."

"Wahoo is expendable."
Lt Commander Dudley Morton, USN.

"He is no fool who gives up what he cannot keep, to gain what he cannot lose."
Jim Elliot (missionary; killed in Ecuador, 1956).

USS Wahoo; July 1943.

16

Do What You Can

"Those who have believed in God
should be careful to maintain good works."
Titus 3:8 (NKJV).

It was after 11 pm and snowing when 29-year-old Mary Forni turned down the street in Hancock, Maine, where she lived. She was driving home from playing cards with friends on that cold November night in 1944. As Mary drove along her street toward home, her headlights shone on two men walking toward her on the side of the road carrying briefcases. Understandably, she didn't stop but instead wondered in quiet amazement at the strangers walking in the snow late at night in this somewhat remote area of Maine.

The two men, Eric Gimpel and William Colepaugh, had just been set ashore at Hancock Point by a U-boat from Nazi Germany's Kriegsmarine. They were spies who had been tasked with making their way to New York City to conduct covert operations and to discover whatever they could about the USA's Manhattan Project. U-1230 had put the spies ashore some 12 miles up Frenchman Bay from the Gulf of Maine and just a short walk from Mary Forni's house.

U-1230 was under the command of Kapitänleutnant Hans Hilbig and departed Norway on October 8, 1944. At that point in the war, Allied anti-submarine forces were sinking U-boats at such a high rate that Hilbig was forced to make nearly the entire crossing to Maine while submerged using a snorkel. The trip took 51 days, but his priority of landing the spies was accomplished.

The following morning, Mary Forni did the only thing she could. She called the local sheriff and reported her sighting of the two men. She discovered that the sheriff's 17-year-old son had also reported seeing the men. Mary and the sheriff's son each contributed to the Allied war effort that day by just doing what they could.

In September 2003, I was on vacation with my family in Bar Harbor, ME. I was familiar with Mary Forni's story and decided to take a drive to Hancock Point to see if there was a marker of some kind where the spies had come ashore. When I got to the town, a group of ladies were talking on the side of the road, so I asked if they knew anything about the spies. I was pleasantly surprised when they said, "Well, Mary Forni lives right over there," pointing to a house down the street.

As we were speaking, Mary pulled into her driveway. I stopped in front of her house and introduced myself. I asked if she could tell me her story regarding the Nazi spies, and she said, "Yes, if you help me carry my groceries into the house." I instantly agreed! After unloading the groceries, Mary directed me to the spot where the spies came ashore on their rubber raft, and she recounted her story. She said that even all these years later, she was still amazed that enemy soldiers from the war in Europe came "so close to my home."

Mary Forni passed away in 2006.

Battle Plan

Soldiers, we are in a war, and in wartime, we all need to do what we can. Maybe you are elderly or disabled in some way and feel you aren't needed or valued in the war effort. Not so!

- Everyone can pray.
- Anyone can reach out on the phone to someone who needs encouragement.
- We can all send a card or make a meal (or use DoorDash).

You might not think it's much, but in God's eyes, it matters very much. Just do whatever you can.

Do not withhold good from those to whom it is due,
when it is in your power to act.
Proverbs 3:27 (NIV)

William Colepaugh (left) and Eric Gimpel

17

Black Hawk Down

*"For what I received, I passed on to you as of first importance:
that Christ died for our sins according to the Scriptures, that
He was buried, that He was raised on the third day according
to the Scriptures."*
1 Corinthians 15:3-4 (NIV).

In 1991-1992, the African country of Somalia was hit with a severe drought that caused critical food shortages. In addition, a civil war was in progress, and the warring factions added to the food shortage by destroying key infrastructure. By early 1992, it was estimated that between 300,000 and 350,000 people had died of starvation. In the summer of 1992, the U.S. became involved in a United Nations multi-national task force that began to deliver essential supplies to the starving nation.

Not surprisingly, the local warlords began commandeering these supplies. As a result of the piracy, the U.S. started sending combat troops along with the supply shipments to protect them from the Warlords. This effort was marginally successful, and by the summer of 1993, the drought, famine, and starvation had largely ended. At that time, the U.N. mission that the United States was leading had transitioned from famine relief to establishing a secure governmental structure. This change was something the warlords would fight hard to prevent.

The most powerful warlord was General Mohammed Farah Aidid. In October 1993, U.S. forces launched a mission to capture Aidid and his top two henchmen. The henchmen were captured, but Aidid escaped. In the process, two Army Black Hawk helicopters were shot down as hundreds of Somali insurgents took to the streets.

One of the downed helicopters was piloted by Chief Warrant Officer Mike Durant, who was injured but alive after the crash. Two Army Delta Force snipers, Sgt. Gary Gordon and Sgt. Randy Shughart asked to be inserted to defend Durant and any possible survivors. Their request was twice denied by their commanding officer, knowing that it would likely be hours before any additional support would arrive on the scene and that the odds of survival were slim. Gordon and Shughart requested permission a third time, and their request was finally granted.

The two snipers were inserted some 300 ft from the crash site and fought their way to the injured pilot. Scores of hostile insurgents surrounded the crash site, and the snipers quickly ran low on ammo as the fighting was intense. Gordon was hit and killed first. Shughart was hit and killed not long after. Pilot Mike Durant was eventually taken prisoner by the insurgents but was released some two weeks later.

Fully aware of what they were doing, Gordon and Shughart willingly gave their lives so that Durant might live.

Battle Plan

Two thousand years ago, the eternal Son of God came to Planet Earth in the person of Jesus Christ and inserted Himself into a fight that wasn't His because we were in a fight we couldn't win. He lived a perfect, sinless life and then willingly gave up that life on the cross so that you and I might live. God accepted the sacrifice of His life as full payment for all the sins of all mankind for all time. He promises to credit that full payment He made on the cross to each person's account the moment they simply believe it.

Yes, it really is that simple.

It really is free, with no fine print and no strings attached. You don't need to raise your hand or fill out a card, you don't need to pray a prayer or walk down an aisle, and you don't need to make a *decision* (the Lord is not appealing to your will. He is appealing to your understanding). I am running a few minutes late; my previous meeting is running over.

What you do need is to be *fully persuaded, fully convinced*, that His promise is true. Soldier, do you believe it? Are you persuaded? If so, tell someone!

"He [Abraham] did not waver through unbelief regarding the promise of God...
being fully persuaded that God had power to do what He had promised."
Romans 4:20-21 (NIV).

Black Hawk Helicopter

GARY MCNALLY

18

"Q" Ships

"But each one is tempted
when he is drawn away by his own desires and enticed.
Then, when desire has conceived, it gives birth to sin,
and sin, when it is full-grown, brings forth death."
James 1:14-15 (NKJV).

On February 13, 1943, the U.S. Submarine Graying was on her fifth war patrol near the Philippine Islands. She approached what appeared to be a small Japanese coastal freighter. The submarine attacked, firing a spread of three torpedoes.

The skipper of the Graying, Lt. Commander John E. Lee, soon discovered that he had been tempted by a "decoy ship" or "Q-Ship." Q-Ships appear to be harmless freighters or transports but have hidden deck guns and depth charges to wage war on submarines that are lured into the trap.

The Q-ship evaded the three torpedoes and quickly turned to retaliate with depth charges. The Grayling was a battle-tested veteran and was able to escape unscathed. As if she didn't already know it, the sub crept away with a fresh reminder that the enemy would love to deceive and destroy her.

The Bible teaches us that God allows trials in the lives of His soldiers to strengthen their faith and to produce endurance. Our enemy, on the other hand, loves to mislead, bringing a temptation into view with the intent to deceive and destroy us. Interestingly, the words *"trial"* and *"temptation"* come from the same word. The key is in the differing intents. God tests us to strengthen us, while Satan tempts us to destroy us. God's intention toward us and His heart for us are always for our good, both here and in the hereafter.

Battle Plan

Speaking for myself, the enemy loves to remind me that *I was born a sinner* (Psalm 51:5). I must also confess that those reminders have, at times, weighed me down. Over the years, it has helped me remember that temptation is not sin.

- Do you have a proneness to a particular temptation or maybe more than one? Me too.
- Has it been in your life for too long? Me too.

Always remember that temptation doesn't become sin until you give in to it. The enemy can't sink you if you don't take the bait, and God always provides a way out.

"God is faithful, Who will not allow you to be tempted beyond what you are able, but with the temptation, will also make the way of escape."
1 Corinthians 10:13 (NKJV).

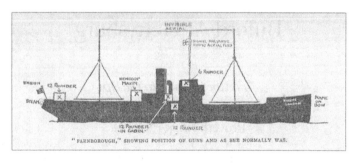

British Q-ship Farnborough
www.historic-uk.com/HistoryUK/HistoryofBritain/Mystery-Ships/

19

Buford At Gettysburg

"The lot is cast into the lap,
but its every decision is from the Lord."
Proverbs 16:33 (NKJV).

When Brigadier General John Buford rode into Gettysburg with his 1st Cavalry Division on the afternoon of June 30, 1863, he had no idea that he was about to make a significant mark on U.S. history. Buford knew that Confederate forces were converging on the town, and he quickly identified the high ground along Cemetery Ridge as crucial should a battle unfold. The Confederate Infantry was approaching from the northwest, so Buford positioned his troops southwest of town near the Lutheran Seminary and stayed the night.

On the morning of July 1, Buford watched from the cupola of the Lutheran Seminary building as his men fought to hold off the forward columns of Confederate General Henry Heath's division, which was trying to enter the town. As the day progressed, Buford was reinforced by the arrival of General John Reynolds' 1st Corps and General Oliver Howard's 11th Corps. Their arrival enabled Buford to gradually withdraw his forces back toward Cemetery Ridge. At the close of fighting on July 1, 1863, Union forces were in command of the high ground along Cemetery Ridge, and John Buford had made his mark on U.S. Military History.

In his second inaugural address, Abraham Lincoln, reflecting on the unfolding events of the Civil War, said, "The Almighty has His own purposes." In saying this, Lincoln identified himself with a large portion of the nation who believed that God was carrying out His purposes and that any human effort to oppose those purposes was futile. God was going to do what God was going to do.

- So, did the Union Army win at Gettysburg because Buford got there first and secured the high ground?
- Or did they win because God was going to do what God was going to do?

In Exodus 17, the Amalekites came and fought against Israel at Rephidim. Moses instructed Joshua to go and fight with the Amalekites while he, Aaron, and Hur stood atop a hill above the battlefield. Moses had the "rod of God" in his hand, and when he extended his arms, the Israelites prevailed. When his arms grew tired and dropped, the Amalekites prevailed. As the battle and the day progressed, Moses' arms grew weary, requiring Aaron and Hur to support his arms, Aaron on one side and Hur on the other. When the day was done, Israel had defeated the Amalekites.

- Was Israel victorious because Aaron and Hur were there to support Moses' arms during the battle?
- Or were they victorious because God was going to do what God was going to do?

Battle Plan

God is indeed sovereign in the affairs of men. It is also true that God uses the plans and endeavors of men to accomplish His will. Our prayer must always be to seek to align our plans with the will of God as best we understand it. Far from wanting God to be on our side, we should always seek to be on His. It seems likely that the answer to all four questions is "yes."

"A man's heart plans his way, but the Lord directs his steps."
Proverbs 16:9 (NKJV).

John Buford Statue at Gettysburg Battlefield,
Rob Shenk, www.battlefield.org

20

Faulty Armor

"Put on the whole armor of God, that you may be able to stand against the wiles of the devil."
Ephesians 6:11 (NKJV).

The use of armor for protection in battle is as old as war itself. For the U.S. Armored Divisions in WW2, the lack of sufficient armor became a major issue. The M4 Sherman tank was designed quickly and mass-produced as the U.S. entered the war.

During the Battle of Normandy, the 3rd U.S. Armored Division suffered the consequences of that hurried design. When an anti-tank projectile hits a tank, it produces incredible energy. If the energy is sufficient to penetrate the tank's shell, it also creates great friction, generating great heat. Hot metal of more than 1000 degrees Fahrenheit would be disbursed inside the stricken tank. With the Sherman, this white-hot metal would sometimes cause the ammo in the tank to ignite, resulting in the complete loss of the tank and often the crew as well.

The British used the Sherman extensively and began referring to it as the "Ronson" tank. Ronson was a popular brand of cigarette lighter soldiers carried during the war, and the company's motto was "It lights up every time." The Germans began referring to the Sherman as the "Tommy Cooker" because their British foes (whom they called "Tommies") often could not escape their tank once it ignited and were "cooked" inside.

German tankers quickly learned the best places to hit the Sherman tanks so that their ammunition supply would likely ignite. Sad to say, the Sherman Tank was not the best example of the kind of armored protection that Allied tankers needed.

In the book of Ephesians, the Apostle Paul makes it clear that Christian soldiers have access to the best armor in the universe.

*"Put on the full armor of God,
so that you can take your stand against the devil's schemes."*
Ephesians 6:11 (NIV).

But, like physical armor, I must be familiar with it and know how to use it. Remember, in 1 Samuel 17, Saul dressed David in his armor before going out to meet Goliath, but David soon realized he wasn't familiar enough with it.

*"Then Saul dressed David in his own tunic.
He put a coat of armor on him and a bronze helmet on his
head. David fastened on his sword over the tunic and tried
walking around because he was not used to them.
"I cannot go in these," he said to Saul, "because I am not used
to them." So, he took them off. "*
1 Samuel 17: 38-39 (NIV).

David hadn't tested the armor, so it wasn't useful to him.
Become familiar with your armor, soldier, and maintain it.
Your spiritual well-being depends on it.

Battle Plan

- Are you a person known to be 'girded' with truth and
  honesty?
- Have you put on the breastplate of righteousness,
  endeavoring to live a consistent, 'righteous' (not perfect)
  life?
- Have you shod your feet with the preparation of the gospel
  of peace so you can clearly share the good news of God's
  amazing grace wherever your feet take you?

Let's be first up and best dressed!

"But let us, who are of the day, be sober,
putting on the breastplate of faith and love,
and as a helmet, the hope of salvation."
1 Thessalonians 5:8 (NKJV).

WW2 Sherman Tank
pierced and destroyed by German anti-tank guns.
https://www.tankroar.com/

21

American Taliban

"A prudent person foresees danger and takes precautions.
The simpleton goes blindly on and suffers the consequences."
Proverbs 22:3 (NLT).

John Walker Lindh is a U.S. citizen, born in Washington, DC, in 1981 and raised in Maryland and California. As a 16-year-old, he converted to Islam, having been heavily influenced by the movie Malcolm X. In 1998, he moved to Yemen for most of that year to take on Islamic Arabic studies. While there, Lindh adopted the name Sulayman al-Faris and, over the next three years, traveled to both Pakistan and Afghanistan. In Afghanistan, he spent time with Al Qaeda and Taliban fighters and is purported to have attended a lecture by Osama bin Laden.

In early 2001, Lindh heard that Taliban forces were in armed conflict with a group known as the Northern Alliance for control of Afghanistan. In May of 2001, he chose to go to Afghanistan to fight with the Taliban. In November 2001, just two months after 9/11, he was captured while fighting with Al Qaeda forces against the Northern Alliance.

When questioned by U.S. Army officials about why he was fighting alongside the group that had just carried out the worst terror attack in U.S. history, Lindh replied that he had wanted to leave his Al Qaeda force after 9/11 occurred but was fearful for his life. He said he never intended to put himself in a position where he could be forced to fight against U.S. forces. At that point, I think the Army interrogator could have asked, "What were you thinking? You shouldn't have been there in the first place!"

Lindh's story is a pointed reminder that soldiers must be careful who they ally themselves with. The Bible tells the story of Jehoshaphat in 2 Chronicles 18. Jehoshaphat was one of the few good kings during the period of the divided kingdom in Israel, but he foolishly allied himself with wicked king Ahab of the northern kingdom. Jehoshaphat's son married Ahab's daughter (Mistake #1), and then the Bible tells us that Jehoshaphat agreed to go to war alongside Ahab to help him reclaim some contested land from the king of Syria (Mistake #2). Ahab had 500 false prophets who told him he would be victorious in the battle. However, there was one true prophet of the Lord, and he indicated that Ahab would be killed in the fight.

As Ahab and Jehoshaphat prepared to enter the battle, Ahab told Jehoshaphat, "*I will disguise myself and go into battle; but you put on your robes*" (2 Chronicles 18:29).

Incredibly, Jehoshaphat agreed, even though this would clearly identify him as a king.

As the battle unfolded, the Syrians, of course, were intent on killing the king of Israel, so they mistakenly went after Jehoshaphat. At this point, Jehoshaphat finally came to his senses. The Bible tells us,

> *"Jehoshaphat cried out, and the Lord helped him, and God diverted them* [Syrian soldiers] *from him."*
> 2 Chronicles 18:31 (NIV).

And despite his disguise, Ahab was killed in the battle.

The natural question would be, 'Jehoshaphat, what were you thinking? You shouldn't have been there in the first place!"

Battle Plan

Christian soldiers need to be very careful who they ally themselves with. When you partner with someone who doesn't share your values and beliefs and they have decision-making powers in the relationship, it can spell disaster. Whether in marriage or business, make sure you are evenly matched.

> *"Do not be yoked together with unbelievers. For what do righteousness and wickedness have in common?*

Or what fellowship can light have with darkness?
What harmony is there between Christ and Belial?
Or what does a believer have in common with an unbeliever?"
2 Corinthians 6:14 (NIV).

22

Grace & War – A Higher Call

"So speak and so do as those who will be judged by the law of liberty. For judgment is without mercy to the one who has shown no mercy. Mercy triumphs over judgment."
James 2:12-13 (NKJV).

The Geneva Conventions are a set of international treaties that establish the fundamental rules of international humanitarian law, particularly in the context of armed conflicts. Its stated purpose is:

"To provide minimum protections, standards of humane treatment, and fundamental guarantees of respect to individuals who become victims of armed conflicts."

In other words, there needs to be some humane boundaries in war. The very nature of war seems to limit the willingness of some to adhere to any boundaries during the war's prosecution. Judeo-Christian ethics seem to wither on the battlefield.

Business and pleasure, oil and water, mercy and war— some things just don't seem to mix well. Yet there was an amazing momentary merging of mercy and war over Nazi Germany on December 20, 1943.

Twenty-one-year-old Lt. Charlie Brown of West Virginia was flying his first combat mission as the pilot of a B-17 bomber, *Ye Olde Pub.* Their target was a factory in one of the best air raid-defended cities, Bremen, Germany. While making their bomb run, *Ye Olde Pub* was literally torn apart by flak and German fighters. Only one of the four engines was running normally, and one was shut down. The rudder was shot to pieces, and the left stabilizer was completely gone. There were two large holes in the plane, four crew members were wounded, and the tail gunner was dead.

Another attack by fighters rendered the oxygen system useless. Shortly after, Charlie and his co-pilot passed out. The plane went into a spiral dive, and at just a few thousand feet above the earth, Charlie woke up. He was able to pull the plane out of the dive and level off just above the snow-covered treetops.

As they fought to maintain control of the aircraft, they passed over a German airfield. BF-109 fighter pilot Franz Stigler was standing next to his plane as the bomber roared by just overhead. Stigler's plane was being refueled and rearmed, and he quickly jumped in and took off after the smoking and badly wounded B-17.

Stigler quickly caught up with *Ye Olde Pub*. As he approached from the rear, he doubtless recalled that he was just one 'kill' away from the coveted Knight's Cross. With his finger on the trigger of his 20 mm cannon, Stigler suddenly saw the bloody body of the tail gunner lying dead over his gun. As he moved up along the right side of the B-17 fuselage, he saw the wounded men inside moving to help each other. He marveled that the plane was still flying, given its ravaged condition.

Instead of shooting the bomber down, Stigler 'escorted' it to the German coast, knowing that flak guns would be hesitant to fire on it with a German fighter plane flying close next to it. When they reached the North Sea coastline, Stigler saluted Lt. Brown and peeled away. *Ye Olde Pub* and its surviving crew members were able to land safely back in England.

The Bible is clear that all believers will stand before the Lord one day to give an account of their service.

> *"For we must all appear before the judgment seat of Christ,*
> *that each one may receive the things done in the body,*
> *according to what he has done, whether good or bad."*
> 2 Corinthians 5:10 (NKJV).

This judgment will determine the extent of our heavenly reward, not our heavenly entrance. Our entrance is secured the very moment we believe in Jesus as our Savior (John 5:24). When the day comes that I stand before the Lord at the believer's judgment, I know I will need mercy. The question is, will there be any?

The Apostle James (our Lord's earthly brother) says it depends. If you have been unmerciful with others during your lifetime, the LORD will show no mercy toward you. But if you have been merciful toward others, then the Lord will be merciful to you.

"Mercy triumphs over judgment."
James 2:13 (NIV).

Battle Plan

There will be just one mitigating factor to help us at the believer's judgment: whatever "stored up" supplies of mercy we might have shown to others.

Store it up now, today, while you can.

Be merciful. Be radically merciful.

You'll be so glad you were.

"Blessed are the merciful, for they will be shown mercy."
Matthew 5:7 (NIV).

"I didn't have the heart to finish those brave men.
I flew beside them for a long time."
-Franz Stigler

B-17 Bomber, Ye Olde Pub, John D. Shaw, Shaw/Valor Studios

23

Communications

"Pray without ceasing."
1 Thessalonians 5:17 (NKJV).

Though their work was usually anonymous, the French Resistance played a crucial part in the success of the D-Day landings in Normandy, France. General William "Wild Bill" Donovan, sometimes called the 'Father of American Intelligence,' once said that 80% of the useful intelligence relevant to the D-Day invasions came from the French Resistance.

Leading up to the Normandy landings, the Resistance had several code-named plans to carry out themselves. At the top of the list were Code Blue (destruction of all power lines) and Code Violet (destruction of all phone lines). The obvious goal was to disrupt or destroy the German Army's ability to communicate. If the enemy can't communicate, how do they pass on information about the size, strength, and positions of the invading Allied Troops? How do they call up troop and armored reinforcements? How do they plan and coordinate counterattacks? Communication is essential.

The Marquis, as the Resistance was called, had significant success in sabotaging German communications, so much so that the 2nd SS Panzer Division was diverted away from the invasion battle and instead served in counter-sabotage efforts.

Communication is no less essential for the Christian Soldier, and the principal means of communication is prayer. Ideally, it is a lifestyle of prayer (communication). The Bible calls it *"pray[er] without ceasing"* (1 Thessalonians 5:17). You might wonder, "How can I pray without ceasing? I have to eat, sleep, and work!"

Understood. We all do. Try thinking of it as constant evaluation. It means going about your everyday life and dealing with everyday problems and issues while at the same time evaluating them through the eyes of our Commander in Chief, Jesus. If we're not in constant contact with Him, how will we react properly to the daily challenges we all face?

Battle Plan

Fellow soldier, our enemy would love to disrupt and destroy our communication lines. Let's start the day by checking in with Headquarters and then keep the lines open all day.

"Personally, I found myself saying a prayer.
It was a prayer that just didn't end."
Major Dick Winters
In preparation for D-Day.

French Resistance in Normandy,
https://www.dday-overlord.com/

GARY MCNALLY

24

Complete Dependence

"Trust in the LORD with all your heart and lean not on your own understanding; in all your ways acknowledge Him, and He shall direct your paths."
Proverbs 3:5-6 (NKJV).

Robert E. Lee is, without question, one of the greatest commanders in military history. He won battle after battle as the commanding general of the Confederate Army of Northern Virginia, often when outnumbered and outgunned.

During the Seven Days Battle of the Peninsula Campaign in 1862, Lee thoroughly intimidated and unnerved the timid commander of the Union Army, George McClellan. Lincoln subsequently cycled through several replacements in his quest to identify an effective leader. His first move was to replace McClellan with General John Pope.

After the Union was crushed at the Second Battle of Bull

Run (also known as the Second Manassas), Lincoln dismissed Pope and brought McClellan back for a second try. When McClellan failed to pursue Lee and the Confederates after the battle of Antietam, Lincoln replaced him with General Ambrose Burnside. After the disastrous Union defeat at Fredericksburg, Lincoln replaced Burnside with General Joe Hooker. When Lee decisively defeated Hooker at Chancellorsville, Lincoln replaced Hooker with General George Meade.

Lincoln's string of hiring and firing was an attempt to find someone – anyone – who would be able to cope with Robert E. Lee. By 1863, Lee was nearly worshiped by the South, and their dependence on him was complete. Then came the Battle of Gettysburg, July 1-3, 1863.

The overall outcome of the first two days of fighting resulted in at least a draw for Lee and the Confederates. But by day three, the Union Army was solidly entrenched on the high ground along Cemetery Ridge, and the Union supply chain was vastly superior to the Confederates. The opinion of Lee's advisors, headed by General James Longstreet, was that they should redeploy to the east toward Washington and either flank the Union position or assume a high-ground position of their own. But as Longstreet later remarked, 'Lee's blood was up.'

On the third day of battle, despite repeated pleas by Longstreet, Lee ordered an attack on the Union center in a desperate attempt to turn the fight in favor of the South. The result was the Confederate disaster we know as Pickett's Charge. In that one attack on the Union lines, the South sustained fifty percent casualties, losing nearly 7000 men in less than an hour of fighting.

Many historians consider Gettysburg to be the turning point of the war. Only a few charging Confederates were able to reach the Union line at a spot called the "Angle" and later, "The High-Water Mark of the Confederacy." The remainder either retreated, were wounded, taken prisoner, or killed in action.

For nearly two more years, it was an outgoing tide for the Confederates all the way to their surrender at Appomattox Court House on April 9, 1865. As Civil War historian Shelby Foote wrote, "Gettysburg was the price the South paid for having R. E. Lee."

Battle Plan

Fellow soldier, if you didn't know it already, people will disappoint you. Your wife or your husband will disappoint you. Your children will disappoint you. Your best friends will disappoint you. The only person who will never disappoint you in the fight for life is Jesus Christ.

That is why He must be your greatest dependency. If you have any dependency that is greater than your dependency on Jesus, it is ultimately an unhealthy dependency. Depend on Jesus, the only Commander who will never disappoint.

FIGHTING FOR LIFE

"It is better to take refuge in the LORD
than to trust in people."
Psalm 118:8 (NLT).

Virginia State Monument, Gettysburg; Lee at the top.
https://www.gettysburgdaily.com/

25

Service Awards

*"... Blessed are the dead who die in the Lord from now on...
That they will rest from their labor,
for their deeds will follow them."*
Revelation 14:13 (NIV).

It has been said that he is the most decorated soldier in
U.S. history. A U.S. Army Green Beret, he served five tours of
duty in Vietnam and was wounded 14 times. His many military
awards include the Medal of Honor (he was nominated three
times), the Distinguished Service Cross, the Silver Star, eight
Purple Hearts, and four Bronze Stars (one for valor).

Robert Lewis Howard was born in Opelika, Alabama, on
July 11, 1939, and entered the U.S. Army a month after
graduating high school on July 20, 1956. His service in special
forces is legendary, and a full list of his service awards would
require more space than we have here. Incredibly, his

numerous medals and accolades don't paint an accurate picture of Howard's combat valor and awareness.

Howard was also part of a special forces team that was frequently assigned cross-border infiltrations into neighboring Cambodia, Laos, and North Vietnam. These missions were normally top secret, and the U.S. military was very reluctant to call attention to them by recognizing soldiers with the highest awards. Howard was nominated for the Medal of Honor two times for such missions, and the nominations were downgraded to the Distinguished Service Cross and the Silver Star because of the secret nature of the mission. Suffice it to say that Howard's service was exceptional. He retired from the army in 1992 as a full Colonel.

Howard served well, and his deeds followed him. After the war, he had innumerable speaking engagements, and a book was written about his life. He was inducted into the Ranger Hall of Fame and had buildings and bridges named after him. He even co-starred with John Wayne in two movies, *The Longest Day* and *The Green Berets*. I'm sure all these things were rewarding for Colonel Howard, but they were also very temporary.

Battle Plan

Fellow soldier, keep in mind that all earthly awards and rewards are temporary. They aren't necessarily wrong; they are just temporal. We might even say they are an illusion simply because they are not eternal and will vanish in an instant. Jesus said;

> "*For whoever wants to save their life will lose it,*
> *but whoever loses their life for Me will save it.*

That is the only saying of Jesus found in all four gospels (Matthew 16:25, Mark 8:35, Luke 9:24, and John 12:25).

Our Lord's words suggest that while we are living *in time*, we would be wise to live *for eternity.* The best awards and rewards we can accumulate in this life are the ones that can only be collected in the life to come.

> "*So, I came to hate life because everything done here under the sun is so troubling. Everything is meaningless—like chasing the wind. I came to hate all my hard work here on earth, for I must leave to others everything I have earned.*"
> Ecclesiastes 2:17-18 (NLT).

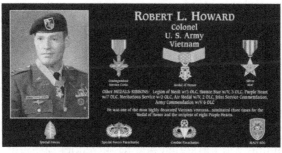

https://soledadmemorial.org/plaques/colonel-robert-l-howard/

26

Hiroo Onoda

"For the message of the cross is foolishness
to those who are perishing."
1 Corinthians 1:18 (NIV).

Toward the end of WW2 in the Pacific, 23-year-old Lieutenant Hiroo Onoda of the Imperial Japanese Army was stationed in the Philippine Islands. In October of 1944, General Douglas MacArthur returned to the Philippines, and the Japanese were in full retreat. In December, a U.S. offensive forced Onoda and his fellow soldiers to retreat into the jungle. Finally, in August of 1945, Japan surrendered, but not Lieutenant Onoda. He fought on, not for weeks or months, but for decades.

Onoda had been selected and trained in guerrilla warfare. His training had forbidden him to surrender or to die by his own hand. He must persevere and fight till the death. He survived in the jungle on bananas, coconuts, insects, and whatever he could 'requisition' from the locals. Onoda refused to make peace with the Philippine culture all around him. He saw all attempts to convince him the war was over as foolishness.

Onoda finally agreed that he would surrender if his commanding officer would come and personally order him to lay down his arms. Major Yoshimi Taniguchi, formerly Onoda's commanding officer, was flown from Japan to the Philippines. At last, in March of 1974, Hiroo Onoda's war finally came to an end.

On the one hand, we may be impressed with Onoda's perseverance and mental toughness. He continued his war for nearly 30 years under very demanding circumstances. On the other hand, Onoda's story is a sad one. He spent decades fighting a war he could never win.

As Christian soldiers, we are surrounded by a world of people who seem intent on fighting a war they can never win on their own. How do we break through to them? How do we persuade them of the truth of the Gospel? How do we reach across cultures with the truth?

In Matthew 19, Jesus encountered a wealthy young man whose opening words showed he was clearly in a "salvation by works" mindset. Jesus challenged him to keep the Mosaic Law (which He knows no one can do). The young man declared that he had kept it "from his youth." Jesus then told him to give his money away to the poor and come follow Him, but the young man was not willing to do that. Why? If he did "love his neighbor as himself," as he had claimed, it wouldn't have mattered to him whether he had his money or his neighbor had it. But clearly, he loved himself at least a little bit more than he loved his neighbor. In His encounter with this young man, Jesus demonstrated to us the importance of meeting people where they are.

Lieutenant Onoda's understanding had been shaped by his culture. It was a culture where obedience, respect, and performance were everything. In his mind, the only way he could end his fight was if his commanding officer ordered him to end it. Thankfully, Major Taniguchi was willing to meet him where he was.

As you reach out with the Gospel of Grace, remember the battle is for the mind.

*"The god of this age has blinded the **minds** of unbelievers so that they cannot see the light of the gospel that displays the glory of Christ, who is the image of God."*
2 Corinthians 4:4 (NIV).

We must be mindful of how culture has shaped a person's thinking. With an approach of prayer and understanding, there is always hope.

———————————

Battle Plan

Rapidly changing cultures, the pervasiveness of relativism, and increasing lawlessness have made evangelism more challenging than ever. There is a need to pray for wisdom, discernment, and guidance at a whole new level. As one contemporary Christian song says, don't stop praying!

Lt. Hiroo Onoda,
https://en.wikipedia.org/wiki/Hiroo_Onoda

27

Hinson's One-Man War

"Do not say, 'I'll do to them as they have done to me;
I'll pay them back for what they did'."
Proverbs 24:29 (cf. Romans 12:19).

Jack Hinson was born in North Carolina in 1807. As a young boy, he moved with his family to Stewart County, Tennessee. He became a farmer and plantation owner in that area, and when the Civil War broke out in 1861, Jack was already in his 50's. He wanted nothing to do with the war. He encouraged his sons to stay neutral and continue working on the family plantation.

For the first year of the war, the Hinsons were able to continue their daily lives with relatively little change. But whatever normalcy they enjoyed would soon end when Union troops under Brigadier General U.S. Grant captured the Confederate-held Fort Donelson in February of 1862. Fort

Donelson was just a few miles from the Hinson Plantation.

The capture of Fort Donelson was a blow to the Confederate cause, and Confederate Guerrillas began a constant series of hit-and-run attacks on Union Troops and supplies coming and going from the fort. The attacks incensed Union Officers to the point where they would send out patrols for the express purpose of capturing anyone suspected of taking part in the guerrilla warfare.

On one such patrol in the fall of 1862, Union Troops came across two of Jack Hinson's sons who were hunting squirrels in the woods near their home. One of the boys was 17, and the other was 21. With no proof, a Union Lieutenant accused the two boys of being guerrillas and executed them on the spot. In one of the most gruesome events of the Civil War, the boys' heads were removed and placed on the fence posts in front of the Hinson Family home.

It goes without saying that Jack Hinson's life was changed forever. The man, whom neighbors and friends described as 'quiet,' became a very different man. He was a man of considerable means, enabling him to pursue a new path. Already known to be an exceptionally good marksman, Hinson ordered a new custom 50 caliber long rifle for the express purpose of long-range killing.

Hinson knew the lieutenant who had murdered his sons as well as the sergeant who had placed the boy's heads on the fence posts. Hinson spent weeks observing the comings and goings of these two officers from Fort Donelson. He also sent his wife and the rest of his family to Western Tennessee to live with relatives. Jack then successfully carried out the killing of both the lieutenant and the sergeant. It didn't take long for Union Officials to realize who had done the deed. Hinson fled the area, and Union forces burned his home to the ground.

Over the next two and a half years, Jack Hinson became one of the most feared snipers in military history, even though his rifle had only iron sights. He spent much of his time in a small cave high on the bluffs above the Tennessee River. From there, he recorded many of his kills of military personnel from Union ships that passed by. Historians believe that many of these kills were made from as far away as 600 yards.

Hinson was never captured despite repeated attempts by Union forces to apprehend him. He survived the war and died of natural causes in 1874. His sniper rifle is still owned by one of his descendants, and it has 36 notches on the barrel, which were cut by Jack Hinson himself. It is believed that the 36 notches represent only the officers that he killed. His total kills are said to be between 80 and 120.

There is no clear indication that Jack Hinson was a man of faith, yet I think it must be admitted that even a man of faith would be capable of reacting as Hinson did to such horrible events. As a father, and given what happened, I can certainly understand his desire for revenge. But as soldiers of Christ, we are held to a very high standard. If we get caught up in temporal endeavors like revenge, pursuit of wealth, or pursuit of power and influence, we will pay the price.

The Judgment Seat of Christ will be a very sobering event for many believers. Our entrance to glory is guaranteed by faith alone in the finished work of Christ on the cross. But we will all stand before Him someday to review our service in His army. The Apostle Paul says our service as Christian Soldiers will be tested by "fire."

Their work will be shown for what it is...
It will be revealed with fire,
and the fire will test the quality of each person's work.
1 Corinthians 3:13 (NIV).

Many Christians think of the Bema Seat (AKA, the Judgment Seat of Christ) as only a positive event for every believer. Not so. Scripture makes it clear that the potential for loss is very real. If we expect to be 'honorably discharged' following the review of our Commander in Chief, we must follow orders.

Battle Plan

Soldiers, going AWOL to fight a war of our own should not be a viable option. Let's stick with the battle plan our Commander has given us. If we are wise, we will leave issues like vengeance to our Commander-in-Chief.

"Vengeance is Mine. I will repay,"says the Lord."
Romans 12:19 (NKJV).

Jack Hinson Monument

28

Dave Roever

"He comforts us in all our troubles so that we can comfort others. When they are troubled, we will be able to give them the same comfort God has given us."
2 Corinthians 1:4 (NLT).

He was born in 1946 and raised in a Christian family in South Texas, near the Mexican border. His father was a preacher, and he has been a believer since childhood. Dave Roever (pronounced Ree-ver) grew up speaking Spanish and English and later learned to speak Vietnamese. He served with SEAL Team #1 as a translator and riverboat gunner in what was known as the 'brown water' navy.

Roever was a 'Black Beret,' patrolling the rivers and coastal areas of Vietnam. It was hazardous duty, and their only real defense was the speed of the boats they patrolled in. Roever had been in Vietnam for eight months when the day came on July 26, 1969, that would change his life forever.

He was about to throw a white phosphorus grenade into a suspected enemy position when a sniper's bullet hit the grenade, igniting it while still in his hand. The resulting explosion covered his upper body with phosphorus, which burns at 5000 degrees Fahrenheit. His first instinct was to jump into the water to douse the fire, but phosphorus cannot be extinguished. It must burn itself out.

Roever would find out later that 60 lbs of skin, muscle, and fat had been burned from his body. Floating in that Vietnamese river, he watched as a large portion of tissue from his body floated next to him. Always intent on keeping his sense of humor, he later remarked, "I was beside myself!" Dave Roever was so severely burned that he spent the next fourteen months in hospitals and underwent fifty-nine surgeries. To this day, his survival is considered a miracle.

In the Bible, in the book of Mark, chapter 5, Jesus and His disciples crossed over to the east side of the Sea of Galilee. There, He encountered a man who was demon-possessed and extremely violent. After casting out the demons, the man was completely restored to his right mind and asked Jesus to allow him to follow Him. Jesus declined and said,

"Go home to your friends,
and tell them what great things the Lord has done for you
and how He has had compassion on you."
Mark 5:19 (NKJV).

Dave Roever did just that. He returned home from Vietnam, and for over 50 years, he has been sharing with people all over the world what the Lord has done for him.

Battle Plan

Remember, soldier, the painful things that have happened to you can be a blessing to others. You have been wounded in war or in life for a reason. It happened so you can encourage and help others. Don't waste your scars!

"But I want you to know, brethren,
that the things which happened to me have actually turned
out for the furtherance of the gospel."
Philippians 1:12 (NKJV).

USN 1142259: U.S. Navy River Patrol Boat, November 1967
Task Force 116 boat moves at high speed down The Saigon River.

29

War On Two Fronts

"I am doing a great work so that I cannot come down."
Nehemiah 6:3 (NKJV).

Many war historians have asked the question, "Was there a single mistake that caused Nazi Germany to lose the second world war?" It is no surprise that there are varying answers to that question, and most have some merit.

Some historians point to the Nazi's failure to vanquish Great Britain in 1940 as the single great mistake. Others say it was Hitler's decision to declare war on the U.S. following Japan's attack on Pearl Harbor in December 1941, when he had no immediate reason to do so. Still, others have said that the tremendous resources the Nazis used to carry out the horrors of the holocaust would have significantly improved Germany's chances in WW2 if they had been used in the war effort instead.

Each of these doubtless contributed to Germany's ultimate defeat. However, if there is one single mistake that cost Germany the war, it was, in this writer's opinion, the mistake they made on June 22, 1941, by invading the Soviet Union.

Germany was already at war with Great Britain in the west. They should have realized that a second front in the east was not a good idea if they just remembered their loss 20 years earlier in WWI while fighting on two fronts. Thankfully for the free world, Hitler and his Nazi thugs decided a war with Britain and a war against the Jews wasn't enough. They needed a war with Russia. If they had even taken the time to survey the sheer manpower that was available to the Soviets, it should have given them pause.

Over the course of World War II, approximately 13 million men served in the German armed forces, while some 35 million men served in Soviet Russia. The Nazis were outnumbered nearly three to one before the fight even started. Whatever slim chance the Nazis had of emerging victorious in WW2, it ended on June 22, 1941.

In 596 BC, Babylon laid siege to Jerusalem, culminating in the city's destruction and the displacement of a large portion of the Israelite population. The prophet Nehemiah (the cup-bearer to King Artaxerxes) prayed that God would soften the King's heart and allow him to return to Jerusalem to rebuild the city walls. God heard Nehemiah's prayers. He returned to rebuild the wall.

Jerusalem West Wall

Once the work was underway, Nehemiah discovered that he had enemies in the persons of Sanballat, Tobiah, and Geshem, who lived in the land and were haters of the Jews (nothing new there). They invented a series of lies about Nehemiah and attempted to lure him into meeting them at a location some distance from Jerusalem. Nehemiah saw the trap and refused to take his eye off the ball. His response is classic: "*I am doing a great work so that I cannot come down.*"

Battle Plan

Fellow soldier, what has the Lord called you to do right now? Whatever it is, you should consider it a *great work!* Self-discipline is critical. Don't come down, and don't get distracted. *Simplify your life.* Guard your schedule as much as possible. Keep a clear eye! Concentrate your forces on the task at hand and avoid the trap of fighting battles on multiple fronts.

*"Let your eyes look straight ahead;
fix your gaze directly before you."*
Proverbs 4:25 (NIV).

30

The Doolittle Raid

"For as he thinks in his heart, so is he."
Proverbs 23:7 (NKJV).

In the weeks and months following the attack on Pearl Harbor in December of 1941, the Japanese also invaded Guam, Wake Island, Hong Kong, the Philippines, Indonesia, Malaya, Singapore, and Burma. The Japanese seemed unstoppable. America was in shock and desperately needed a battlefield victory to restore morale and get her people thinking right again.

A very daring and unorthodox plan was devised to launch 16 Army B-25 Mitchell Bombers from the deck of a U.S. aircraft carrier to bomb Tokyo and the Japanese mainland. Colonel James "Jimmy" Doolittle recruited 80 men and then personally planned and led the mission. On April 18, 1942, Doolittle and his men launched earlier than intended from the

U.S. Carrier Hornet after being sighted by a Japanese vessel. Instead of being 400 miles from Japan as planned, they were 650 miles but decided to launch anyway. The "highly dangerous" mission was starting to look like a suicide mission with doubtful fuel sufficiency.

All 16 planes successfully took off from the Hornet, and all 16 dropped their bombs on Japan. Through a set of unique circumstances, including an unexpected tailwind, 15 planes made it to the coast of China (ditching when out of fuel), and one landed in Russia. 71 of the 80 men, including Doolittle, returned safely to the USA. Damage to the Japanese war industry was not great, but the damage to Japanese morale and the change in Japanese thinking was enormous.

The meaning of Proverbs 23:7 is that what we think about and how we think about it will tend to show up in our lives and actions. Think of human cognition as a steam engine. Circumstances produce the spark of ignition. Ignition produces the fires of thought. The fires of thought produce the steam of action. *"As a man thinks, so is he."*

The Doolittle Raid humiliated Japan's military leaders, significantly influencing their thinking regarding military strategy. In response, they formulated a plan to establish a "buffer" zone between the Japanese home islands and U.S. naval forces in Hawaii. Their decision led to a plan to attack and capture Midway Island.

Many historians have pointed out that Japan's devastating defeat at the Battle of Midway in June 1942 was the direct result of that change in thinking by the Japanese high command, resulting from the Doolittle Raid just two months earlier. The defeat at Midway turned the tide of World War II against the Japanese Empire.

Battle Plan

Fellow soldier, be very careful what you set your eyes and ears on. Take care of what you think about and how you think about it. The desired outworking of our faith can only come from a prayerful and well-disciplined mind.

> *"...we take captive every thought*
> *to make it obedient to Christ."*
> 2 Corinthians 10:5 (NIV).

"If we should have to fight, we should be prepared to do so from the neck up instead of from the neck down."
Jimmy Doolittle

Mitchell Bombers ready for Doolittle Raid,
Source: Wikimedia Commons, License: Public Domain.

31

Smart Bombs

"Devote yourselves to prayer, being watchful and thankful."
Colossians 4:2 (NIV).

Saddam Hussein's Iraqi army invaded Kuwait on August 2, 1990. Five months later, on January 17, 1991, US-led Coalition forces launched a massive air campaign against Iraqi targets. For five weeks, coalition air power was brought to bear on Iraq's military infrastructure with brutal strength and precision.

When the ground offensive began on February 24, 1991, the dictator was still defiant. He famously declared that the coming conflict would be "the mother of all battles." Iraq indeed boasted a substantial military, with an estimated one million personnel in uniform. Of those, about 360,000 were army ground troops. They were estimated to have 5,000 tanks and 3800 pieces of artillery. On paper, the Iraqi military was, in fact, one of the largest in the world. Yet when the ground campaign began, it took only four days for the Coalition forces to completely subdue the Iraqis. Operation Desert Storm would become known as the '100 Hour War.'

What happened? How did 'the mother of all battles' so quickly become a total rout? In truth, the coalition forces were superior to the Iraqis in tactics, leadership, training, and technology. In the battle itself, the technology factor was decisive. From aircraft to armored vehicles to bombs, coalition forces had the most advanced weapons ever used in warfare.

One such weapon was the smart bomb. In past wars, a bomb was dropped from a plane and simply fell to the ground. Once released, there was no further control or guidance possible. This type of bomb has more recently been referred to as a 'dumb bomb.' If the target was a factory, the hope was that the bomb would hit it.

With a smart bomb, it is guaranteed that the factory will be hit. The only question was, which specific part of the factory do you want to impact? Do you want to send it in through one of the skylights? No problem. Want it to enter through the front door? We can do that too. Smart bombs were both crucial and decisive in the Coalition's effort to oust the Iraqis from Kuwait.

In the book of Nehemiah, we read that Nehemiah, who served as cupbearer to Persian King Artaxerxes, learned that the city and walls of Jerusalem were in ruins. He was heartbroken and desired to return to Jerusalem and rebuild the city walls. As he served the king, the king noticed Nehemiah's sad countenance and asked, "Why is your face sad, though you are not ill?" Nehemiah explained that he was downcast because the city where his ancestors lived was in ruins.

The king answered, "What is your request?" At this point, Nehemiah needed to be very careful. A sour (or sad) expression was not normally permitted in the king's presence, much less the asking of a favor. The Bible tells us what Nehemiah did next, "So I prayed to the God of heaven" (Nehemiah 2:4). Smart move! Nehemiah then requested to return and rebuild the walls of Jerusalem. The king said yes!

Battle Plan

Soldier, what is your first resort under stress? With his life on the line and only seconds to respond, Nehemiah PRAYED! No doubt a silent prayer and only a few words, but he prayed! Soldiers engaged in spiritual warfare possess a 'smart bomb' that is always at their disposal and always hits its target. It instantly brings the Commander-in-Chief to the forefront. And take it from Nehemiah. The smart bomb prayer doesn't need a long fuze (yes, fuze, not fuse).

The prayer of a righteous person is powerful and effective.
James 5:16b (NIV)

"Life is 10% what happens to you
and 90% how you react to it."
Chuck Swindoll.

Smart Laser-Guided Bomb,
https://en.wikipedia.org/wiki/Laser-guided_bomb

32

In His Shadow

"A thousand may fall at your side, and ten thousand at your right hand; but it shall not come near you."
Psalm 91:7 (NKJV).

Known to be a devout man of prayer, George Washington was born in Virginia in 1732. Also known as "the father of our country," he has a history more remarkable than most Americans are aware of.

Washington's military exploits began twenty years before the American Revolution, during the French and Indian War. In the summer of 1755, British General Edward Braddock was to move westward from Virginia to attack and take the French Fort Duquesne near present-day Pittsburgh, PA. Only twenty-three years old at the time, Washington received and accepted an invitation to join Braddock's expedition as a member of his staff.

Washington would later discover that Braddock was long on courage but short on humility. As they slowly cut their way through the wilderness, Indian scouts and Washington both warned Braddock of the possibility of an ambush. He brushed the warnings aside, believing that the French and their Indian allies were no match for British Regulars. On July 9, 1755, Braddock's army was ambushed by the French and Indians in what would later become known as the Battle of Monongahela.

The British were completely unprepared for the tactics of the French and Indians. They fired from behind rocks and trees, and it became a slaughter. The British suffered sixty percent casualties. Sixty-three of the approximately 85 British officers (which included Washington) were killed in action, including Braddock, who was mortally wounded.

With Braddock out of the fight, Washington became a key player. He moved over every corner of the battlefield. By the end of the fight, Washington had two horses shot out from under him and multiple bullet holes in his uniform. His physician and friend, Dr. James Craik, was present at the battle and later wrote,

"I expected every moment to see him fall.
His duty and station exposed him to every danger.
Nothing but the superintending care of Providence could
have saved him from the fate of all around him."

In a letter to his brother John, Washington later wrote that he had been protected "beyond all human probability or expectation."

In 1770, fifteen years after the battle, Washington and Dr Craik met with one of the Indian chiefs who had fought with the French that day. Statesman and historian George Bancroft recorded that the chief said,

"Our rifles were leveled – rifles which,
but for him [Washington], knew not how to miss. 'Twas all in
vain; a power far mightier than we shielded him from harm.
He cannot die in battle..."
Faith & Freedom, Benjamin Hart

The Indian Chief's words were prophetic. Washington survived the Revolutionary War and several other close calls. In 1777, before the Battle of Brandywine commenced, Washington rode out to survey the battlefield. He rode into a field, not knowing that a company of British sharpshooters was concealed in the woods. The group was led by Captain Patrick Ferguson, a man purported to be the best shot in the British Army. Ferguson initially gave the order to shoot the colonial officer. But then said, 'Something didn't feel right.' He canceled the order, and Washington rode away.

————————————

Battle Plan

Think back for a minute.

- Did the Lord deliver Elijah from Ahab and Jezebel?
- Did He deliver Daniel from the lions?
- Did He deliver David from homicidal King Saul?

Yes, and He will deliver you, too.

Remember, the greatest deliverance is when we are delivered from this world into the world to come!

"And the Lord will deliver me from every evil work and preserve me for His heavenly kingdom."
2 Timothy 4:18 (NKJV).

"The Prayer at Valley Forge."
Engraving by John McCrae, based on the painting by Henry Brueckner, ca. 1889. John C. McRae/Library of Congress.

33

Early Warning Systems

*"Since they heard the sound of the trumpet but did not heed
the warning, their blood will be on their own head.
If they had heeded the warning,
they would have saved themselves."*
Ezekiel 33:5 (NIV).

The Japanese attack on Pearl Harbor in December 1941
was, for my parents' generation, what 9/11 was for Gen Z'ers.
Both of my parents remembered exactly where they were and
what they were doing when they first heard of the attack.
Growing up, I was always told the United States had no
warning of the Pearl Harbor attack. While that was mostly
true, it wasn't entirely true.

In the late 1930's, the U.S. military began experimenting
with RADAR, an acronym for Radio Detection and
Ranging. One such early radar unit was set up on

Thanksgiving Day, November 20, 1941, at Opana Point on the north shore of the Island of Oahu in Hawaii. On the morning of December 7, 1941, the new radar station was manned by Army privates Joseph Lockard and George Elliot. At 7:02 am, the two men saw a very large blip on the screen and reported the following,

"Large number of planes coming in from the north.
Three points east."

The planes they detected were 137 miles north of Oahu, and unknown to the men, they were Japanese planes. They sent their report up the chain of command but were told by duty officer Lt. Kermit Tyler, "Don't worry about it."

To be fair, on that historic morning in 1941, radar was in its infancy. Lockard and Elliot were both just learning the basics of the new technology. The first time looking at a radar scope is daunting for anyone. In addition, Lt. Tyler was in his first week of training and was aware of a flight of U.S. Army B-17 bombers flying in that morning from California, and those bombers would be approaching Oahu from the north. While all three men might have done better in their circumstances, their reactions were understandable because *the information they had wasn't sending them a clear message.*

I grew up a Roman Catholic, and ever since I first understood and believed the Gospel of Grace in March of 1980, it has been the passion of my life and ministry to send a clear message.

Being in a right relationship with God has been described in various ways;

- Receiving eternal life.
- Being saved
- Becoming a member of God's forever family.
- Getting into heaven.
- Justification by faith

Label it whatever you will. Eternal life is an absolutely FREE GIFT, given by God's grace, and it is received by faith alone in Christ alone, plus NOTHING. When I came to understand and believe that truth in 1980, it changed my life forever. I know it can change yours, too.

*"For God so loved the world that He gave His one and only Son, that whoever **believes** in Him shall not perish but have eternal life."*
John 3:16 (NIV).

Battle Plan

Believing that Jesus' death has paid your sin debt in full is ALL that God requires. Do you believe that?

Are you fully persuaded?
If you are, *tell someone!*

"Now to the one who works, wages are not credited as a gift

*but as an obligation. However, to the one who **does not work**
but trusts God who justifies the ungodly, their faith [belief] is
credited as righteousness."*
Romans 4:4-5 (NIV).

Opana Point Radar, Oahu
Pearl Harbor Chamber of Commerce.

34

The May Incident

"Death and life are in the power of the tongue..."
Proverbs 18:21 (NKJV).

For a U.S. Submarine in the Pacific during WW2, nothing was more dangerous and terrifying than being subjected to an enemy depth charge attack. Most Japanese merchant ship convoys were accompanied by Imperial Japanese Navy (IJN) destroyers, who were only too happy to unleash a barrage of depth charges on any U.S. submarine that dared to threaten their convoy.

In the first eighteen months of the war, U.S. submarines were generally successful in surviving depth charge attacks, partly due to the Japanese reliance on outdated intelligence. The Japanese approach to depth charge attacks was based on World War I-era U.S. submarines, which had a maximum test depth of 200 feet. WW2 Gato Class submarines had a maximum test depth of 300 ft, and WW2 Balao Class submarines had a maximum test depth of 400 ft. As a result, Japanese depth charges tended to explode well above the U.S. subs.

In June 1943, Congressman Andrew May of Kentucky had just returned from a tour of the Pacific Theater of Operations. In a press conference, he announced that our submarine forces in the Pacific were conducting a successful campaign against Japanese shipping. He also mentioned that even when attacked by Japanese destroyers, our submarines would usually escape because the Japanese depth charges were set to explode at rather shallow depths. Newspapers, of course, published May's remarks, and by the fall of 1943, the Japanese had adjusted their depth charges.

Vice Admiral Charles A. Lockwood, Commander of US Pacific Submarine Forces (COMSUBPAC), said,

> "I hear Congressman May said the Japanese depth charges are not set deep enough. He would be pleased to know they are setting them deeper now."

Admiral Lockwood later estimated that ten U.S. Subs and 800 officers and crew were lost because of Congressman May's loose tongue.

The Book of Proverbs says that the mouth of a fool *invites a beating* (Proverbs 18:6). Tragically, the Congressman's foolish mouth resulted in a fatal beating for hundreds of U.S. Submariners. I have found that controlling my tongue is one of the greatest challenges in my life as a Christian soldier. My words might not have caused anyone to lose their life, but my words have, at times, caused pain even to people I love. In the battle of the Christian life, it is sometimes wise to keep your opinion to yourself and always wise to remember that there are some things that should never be repeated.

Battle Plan

Think twice (or three times) the next time you are tempted to voice your opinion or 'share' something of a sensitive nature or something about a fellow soldier. A careless tongue doesn't just hurt individuals. It can bring aid and comfort to the enemy. In war, loose lips really can sink ships.

"Tell it not in Gath;
repeat it not in the streets of Ashkelon."
2 Samuel 1:20

Depth Charge Attack, WWII.
https://www.warhistoryonline.com/

35

Wrongly Accused

*"When He [Christ] was reviled, He did not revile in return;
when He suffered, He did not threaten but
committed Himself to Him who judges righteously."*
1 Peter 2:23 (NKJV).

During the Civil War, Confederate General Richard B.
Garnett was, by implication, accused of cowardice by his
commanding General, Thomas "Stonewall" Jackson. Jackson
relieved Garnett of command and pressed charges against
him after he ordered his brigade to retreat from the battlefield
at the First Battle of Kernstown on March 23, 1862. Post-battle
intelligence revealed that Garnett had been instructed to
attack Union forces based on faulty information (the Union's
actual strength was twice what had been reported, and
Garnett's men were low on ammunition and surrounded on
three sides). It was clear that his decision to withdraw was

entirely justified.

A few months after the battle, General Robert E. Lee ordered Garnett reinstated to command a brigade under General George Pickett. Due to pressing matters of the war, Garnett's full court martial was delayed, and when General Jackson was killed at the battle of Chancellorsville in April of 1863, the court martial was destined to never happen. Garnett rightly felt he had been falsely accused. However, being accused by an officer like Stonewall Jackson was enough to make anyone feel like they were guilty, whether they were or not.

Over the following year, fellow officers observed Garnett to be itching for an opportunity to vindicate himself. The assignments of his brigade did not afford him that opportunity until July 1863 at the Battle of Gettysburg.

Before the battle, Garnett was badly injured by a horse kick to his leg. By the time of the fight, he was unable to walk any distance and was running a fever, likely from the leg injury. Despite being urged by fellow officers not to make the attack later known as Pickett's Charge, Garnett insisted. Unable to walk, he elected to make the charge on horseback, clearly making him a prime target.

Garnett was able to survive the Union artillery barrage unscathed as he crossed the nearly one-mile distance from Seminary Ridge to Cemetery Ridge. Some witness testimony placed him within 50 yards of the Union lines at the Bloody Angle. Shortly thereafter, however, Garnett was killed. It was likely by canister fire or grapeshot since his remains were never identified.

How does a soldier survive being wrongly accused? When you are committed to a cause and have fully given yourself to it, nothing could be more painful than being accused of somehow betraying that cause. In Genesis chapter 39, Joseph was falsely accused of sexual impropriety and then imprisoned. Given Joseph's character, it is unlikely that the imprisonment was the most difficult consequence for him to accept. More likely, the pain of being accused of something he never did was the most difficult burden to bear.

Fellow soldier, have you ever been accused of something you never did? Me too. Remember that we are serving the One who made Himself of *no reputation* (Philippians 2:7). Why are we so concerned about ours?

Battle Plan

Joseph was later vindicated by the Lord's direct intervention, but not all who are wrongly accused will be so blessed. Sometimes, you just have to thank the Lord for the privilege of suffering for Him and wait for His ultimate vindication. It may not come here, but it will absolutely come hereafter.

"Blessed are you when they revile and persecute you and say all kinds of evil against you falsely for My sake.

FIGHTING FOR LIFE

Rejoice and be exceedingly glad,
for great is your reward in heaven."
Matthew 5:11-12 (NKJV).

Union and Confederate survivors of Pickett's Charge shake hands at the Bloody
Angle; 50-year reunion, 1913.
https://civilwarstuff.com/

36

O Captain! My Captain!

"For it became Him, for whom are all things, and by whom are all things, in bringing many sons unto glory, to make the captain of their salvation perfect through sufferings."
Hebrews 2:10 (KJV).

When Confederate General Robert E. Lee surrendered the Army of Northern Virginia at Appomattox Court House on April 9, 1865, no one had greater reason to celebrate than Abraham Lincoln, who learned of the surrender that evening.

Lincoln had worked very long hours for four long years, and the war had taken its toll on him. Still, he was somewhat subdued upon receiving the news. His mind had already shifted towards planning a "let them up easy" post-war policy toward the South that would hopefully help to heal the nation's wounds.

The following day, when a jubilant crowd assembled at the White House, they persuaded the President to make a few remarks from an open window. Noticing there was a band present, Lincoln requested they play 'Dixie,' demonstrating his mindset of reconciliation. Just four days later, Lincoln would be dead.

American poet Walt Whitman served as a nurse for recovering Union Soldiers during the war, and he greatly admired Lincoln. Whitman's younger brother, George, had served in the Union Army, and when he was wounded at Fredericksburg, the elder Whitman had traveled to Virginia to nurse him back to health. Like many Americans, Whitman was deeply affected by Lincoln's death and penned his famous poem "O Captain! My Captain!" in 1865. The poem portrays the nation as a ship, symbolizing the Union, with Lincoln as its captain. The final verse of the poem reads:

My Captain does not answer.
His lips are pale and still,
My father does not feel my arm.
He has no pulse, nor will,

The ship is anchor'd safe and sound,
Its voyage closed and done,
From fearful trip, the victor ship
comes in with object won;

Exult, O shores, and ring, O bells!
But I, with mournful tread,
Walk the deck, my Captain lies,
Fallen, cold, and dead.

After four years of the bloodiest war in American history, with the fighting "closed and done," America's 'captain' had saved the Union. Then, tragically, he was assassinated on Good Friday, 1865.

1800+ years earlier, on Good Friday circa 33AD, the Captain of our salvation laid down His life that you and I might live. *He is the atoning sacrifice for our sins, and not only for ours but also for the sins of the whole world.* (1 John 2:2 NIV). He was crucified and buried, and three days later, He rose from the dead. His substitutionary sacrifice doesn't just save a nation. It saves everyone in the world who simply believes.

The Captain of our salvation is alive! He was slain for us, but He lives! Think about that, soldier. It isn't only a matter of faith; it is a fact of history. Depend on it!

Battle Plan

The forces of evil and my own sin may have put Jesus in the grave, but He didn't stay there. Our Captain lives, and He is always there to guide and direct, to comfort and console, to cleanse, and to encourage.

Have you believed in Him? Are you calling on Him?

"Therefore, He is also able to save to the uttermost those who
come to God through Him,
since He always lives to make intercession for them."
Hebrews 7:25 (NKJV).

"I will call on Him as long as I live."
Psalm 116:2 (NIV).

He is risen.

37

Suffering In Hope

"... We also glory in tribulations, knowing that tribulation produces perseverance; and perseverance, character, and character, hope. Now hope does not disappoint..."
Romans 5:3-5 (NKJV).

On November 15, 2023, America lost an icon of hope at the age of 102. Lloyd Ponder, the oldest of five brothers, was born on October 12, 1921, in Louisiana. He graduated first in his high school class in 1938, but during the Depression, money for college was scarce. Always mechanically inclined, he enlisted in the Army Air Corps and became an airplane mechanic. His unit arrived in the Philippines just a week before the Japanese attack on Pearl Harbor in 1941.

Shortly after, the Japanese invaded the Philippines, and Ponder found himself fighting with the infantry. Outnumbered and on the defensive against the invaders,

Ponder and his fellow soldiers were cut off from supply lines and were soon forced to kill and eat horses and mules to survive. In April 1942, the province of Bataan fell. Ponder narrowly evaded capture and the resulting Bataan Death March. Physically and mentally exhausted from hunger, malaria fevers, and constant artillery shelling, Ponder successfully escaped to Corregidor and fought alongside U.S. Marines until the island surrendered. He became a POW in May of 1942.

For the next three years and beyond, Ponder endured a nightmare. For two years, he was held in POW camps in the Philippines. Then, in the summer of 1944, he was crammed into a ship's cargo hold with no sanitation facilities along with sixteen hundred other POWs for the two-week voyage to Japan. In an interview in early 2023, Ponder recalled looking down into the hold as he boarded the ship. He said, "It made me think I was having a nightmare." His final year as a POW was spent working in a factory in Japan under horrific conditions. When Japan finally surrendered in August 1945, Lloyd Ponder weighed just 90 lbs.

As a Christian man speaking of his ordeal, Ponder said, "I made a habit of daily prayer. When everything appeared hopeless, I'm certain God sustained me." He also said that the greatest miracle from his perspective is, "When I got out, I didn't have a scratch anywhere. That's a miracle!" Lloyd Ponder knew the Lord was in control, no matter how out of control the situation seemed to be.

No human suffering can ever compare to the suffering of the Lord Jesus at Calvary. Yet, amid even that, the Bible tells us that His Father was in total control and *"not one of His bones shall be broken."* (Psalm 34:20, John 19:31-33, 36).

Battle Plan

Fellow soldier, keep in mind that physical deliverance on earth is always partial. We will never be completely pain-free in this world. But no matter what is happening in your life right now, remember this: Not a mark (physical or emotional) can be put on your body, and not one of your bones can be broken unless your Lord allows it. He is in absolute control. Count on Him. Call on Him.

"Whosoever shall call on the name of the LORD shall be delivered."
Joel 2:32 (KJV)

"Many are the afflictions of the righteous, but the Lord delivers him out of them all."
Psalm 34:19 (NKJV).

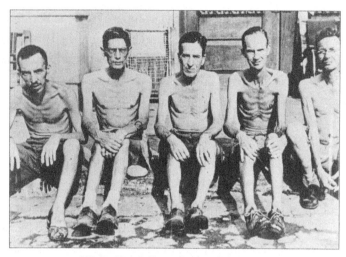

Allied soldiers held in a Japanese POW Camp.
Image credit: NPS/ANDE.

38

Hero Without a Gun

"Blessed are you when people insult you, persecute you, and falsely say all kinds of evil against you because of Me.
Rejoice and be glad,
because great is your reward in heaven..."
Matthew 5:11-12 (NIV).

When he joined the U.S. Army in April of 1942, twenty-three-year-old Desmond Doss little knew what he was in for. He was a devout Christian and had grown up as a Seventh-Day Adventist. He promised God as a young boy that he would never take a human life. He assumed that, as a conscientious objector and a combat medic, he would not be required to carry a firearm. He was assuming too much. When Doss refused to pick up a gun in basic training, he was ridiculed by officers and fellow soldiers alike. When persevered in his convictions, the hazing and verbal abuse progressed to physical abuse. One fellow soldier even threatened to kill him.

Convinced that he would be a liability in combat situations, the Army wanted him gone. They tried to dismiss him as mentally ill. They attempted to court-martial him and even jailed him for a time. All their efforts eventually failed, and in the summer of 1944, Doss found himself doing what he had wanted to do all along: serve his country as a combat medic while not carrying a gun.

Doss served with distinction in both Guam and the Philippines and was awarded the Bronze Star in both locations. While under enemy fire, he treated the wounds of the same men who had ridiculed and abused him. In May 1945, he saved the lives of seventy-five of his wounded comrades at the battle of Hacksaw Ridge on the island of Okinawa. For his heroism, Desmond Doss was awarded the Medal of Honor.

Perhaps the most amazing thing happened just before the final battle for Hacksaw Ridge on May 5, 1945. The men of Doss's unit were reluctant to go into the final day of fighting without him. With their commanding officer's consent, they chose to delay engaging the enemy, instead waiting several hours for Doss to finish reading his Bible and praying. He had gone from outcast to hero.

The Bible tells us about two other devout believers in the God of Israel who were forced into foreign environments: Joseph, who was sold into slavery in Egypt, and Daniel, who was taken into exile in Babylon. Both men refused to compromise their moral standards. Both men initially made enemies and were persecuted and punished for their ethical stances. Yet, both were eventually vindicated, rewarded, and ultimately respected.

Sound familiar? Joseph, Daniel, and Desmond Doss each demonstrated that courage, forgiveness, and self-sacrifice are irresistibly powerful virtues and that God will invariably vindicate His people.

Battle Plan

If you find yourself facing persecution for standing up for what is right, don't waver in your convictions. Don't change course. Take a moment for an attitude check, stay gracious, and trust the Lord regarding the outcome. You will be eternally happy you did.

"For the Lord will vindicate His people
and have compassion on His servants."
Psalm 135:14 (NIV).

Desmond Doss atop the escarpment at Hacksaw Ridge, May 4, 1945.
Photo courtesy of the US Army.

39

Pearl Harbor

"Shall we accept good from God and not trouble? "
Job 2:10 (NIV).

When Japanese air and naval forces attacked the United States at Pearl Harbor on December 7, 1941, it was a shock unlike any our nation had ever known. Yes, there were ongoing tensions with Japan. Yet without a declaration of war or even a threat of imminent hostilities, the Japanese carried out a devastating surprise attack that killed 2400 Americans and wounded hundreds more.

A member of the Greatest Generation once told me that the first week or two following the attack felt like a scene from a movie: a soldier caught in the chaos of battle is severely impacted by an explosion, and while still conscious and aware of their surroundings, everything around them is eerily silent and in slow motion.

Completely stunned, America was trying to make sense of what had happened and wondering how to proceed. The Japanese military strategists were relying on the shock and devastation caused by the Pearl Harbor attack to completely demoralize the American people, hoping they would want to immediately sue for peace. But as history would show, they were badly mistaken.

In the oldest book of the Bible, we read the story of a man named Job. He was richly blessed by God with material possessions and enjoyed a close relationship with Him. Yet, in a curious turn of events, God allowed Satan to test Job in any way he desired, short of killing him. Satan challenged God, asserting that if Job suffers such afflictions, he will surely "*curse You to Your face!*" (Job 2:5, NKJV).

Satan's first attack took the lives of all of Job's children and destroyed all his wealth and possessions. Satan then devastated Job's health by covering his body with painful boils "*from the sole of his foot to the crown of his head*" (Job 2:7, NKJV).

In the boxing realm, it is said that "everyone has a plan until they get punched in the face." The Japanese were hoping that the sucker punch at Pearl Harbor would cause the U.S. to immediately throw in the towel. Satan believed that the savagery and shock of his attack on Job and his family would cause him to turn against God. Japan and Satan had one thing in common: they both underestimated their victims.

Battle Plan

None of us knows what kind of challenge or adversity today will bring. Life can be very unpredictable. No matter what challenges today may bring, I pray that you and I will demonstrate that we are made of better stuff than our adversary realizes.

"If you faint in the day of adversity, your strength is small."
Proverbs 24:10 (NKJV).

Battleship Row at Pearl Harbor after the attack, with capital ships settling on the bottom, December 1941. U.S.S Arizona (center), U.S.S Tennessee (left), and the sunken U.S.S West Virginia.

Official U.S. Navy Photograph, from the collections of the Naval History and Heritage Command. NH 97378

40

Precious Time

"Teach us to number our days,
that we may gain a heart of wisdom."
Psalm 90:12 (NIV).

Thirty-two-year-old Todd Beamer had planned to fly to California on the evening of September 10, 2001, but decided instead to fly on the morning of September 11 so he could spend the extra time with his wife and two sons. As he boarded United Flight 93 in Newark, NJ, that morning, he had no way of knowing that he and his fellow passengers would soon be fighting the first battle in the War on Terror and that today would be his last day on earth.

Todd and his wife Lisa were both evangelical Christians and had met when they were students at Wheaton College ten years earlier.

Lisa would later recall the fateful morning of September 11, 2001:

"I was standing behind my couch. I'll always remember when I heard them say that it was the United flight from Newark to San Francisco that just went down..."

In that instant, Lisa realized it was Todd's plane.

Just a short time earlier, Flight 93 had been hijacked by Islamic terrorists. Using phones, Todd and his fellow passengers discovered that other hijacked planes had already crashed into the World Trade Center in Manhattan and the Pentagon in Washington, DC. They understood that their plane was very likely part of a larger planned attack on the USA. After praying the Lord's Prayer, Todd took the initiative to lead his fellow passengers in retaking control of the aircraft. His final known words are familiar to most Americans: "Let's roll."

Like countless others who would lose loved ones that day, Lisa was faced with profound grief and an uncertain future as a single parent. She would later share some of her thoughts in her 2003 book, *Let's Roll.*

Any honest believer might question why the Lord had allowed Todd to be on Flight 93, especially since he had only delayed his departure in order to spend time with his family. William Cowper's words, written 250 years ago, still ring true.

God moves in a mysterious way,
His wonders to perform.
He plants his footsteps in the sea
And rides upon the storm...
When tears are great and comforts few,
We hope in mercies ever new.
We trust in You.

Starting with the Revolutionary War, citizen soldiers have been a catalyst in the quest for American freedom. Lisa Beamer could take solace in the fact that her husband stood with great courage not only in defense of his earthly country and freedom but, more significantly, his actions pointed to his first allegiance: his heavenly citizenship and eternal freedom.

Battle Plan

The Bible tells Christians not to grieve *"as those who have no hope"* (1 Thessalonians 4:13). What makes the difference for Christians? The difference is time. If it is possible to simplify grief, it may be that the core of grief is that we simply run out of time. Todd Beamer wisely understood that his time with his family here on earth was limited, and he chose to maximize it.

Very soon, for believers, limited time won't be an issue.

"[Make] the best use of the time because the days are evil."
Ephesians 5:16 (ESV)

Flight 93 Memorial, Shanksville, P.A.

Conclusion
The Spirit of 2026

*"For our struggle is not against flesh and blood, but against
the rulers, against the authorities, against the powers of this
world's darkness, and against the spiritual forces of evil
in the heavenly realms."*
Ephesians 6:12 (NIV).

On March 20, 2025, President Donald Trump issued a proclamation commemorating the 250th anniversary of Patrick Henry's speech to the Second Virginia Convention in March of 1775. Henry famously ended his speech with the words, "Give me liberty or give me death."

In his speech, Patrick Henry also said, "If we wish to be free... we must fight!" His words are true, but they can also, I believe, be a trap for Christian soldiers. I confess to being a patriot who would fight for my country with arms if it came to that. However, the older I get, the more I realize that as a believing soldier, the vast majority of my fighting must be done with a focus on my heavenly citizenship rather than on my US citizenship. I have found over the years that I can all too easily fall into the trap of trying to fight with harsh words and political polemics rather than fighting with empathy and prayer.

- Are my political opinions still there? Of course.
- Do I still think to myself, 'How stupid are you!' when I see certain bumper stickers on a car? Yep.

I can't always help how I feel, but I can help what I do about the way I feel. The Spirit of God whispers, 'Don't disparage that person. If you think they are wrong, pray for them!'

In writing these devotional thoughts, I have sought to point out the ways that physical warfare and spiritual warfare are similar. But the two are and must be very dissimilar regarding the weapons and attitudes that are used to fight them.

When Patrick Henry rose to address his fellow Virginians in March of 1775, his words were intended to incite them to arms and to fight for freedom. The great advantage of Christian soldiers is that we know our freedom has already been secured. By His death, burial, and resurrection, Jesus Christ has won our eternal freedom. However, until our Commander returns, the forces of evil are still active, so we must fight. But remember, our fight is spiritual in nature, using spiritual weapons: prayers and petitions rather than guns and grenades.

On July 4, 2026, our nation will celebrate its 250th birthday. There will doubtless be some very big celebrations and commemorations across the country. As someone who feels blessed to be a citizen of this great land, I'm looking forward to it. But I'm also hoping that it will be a time of soul-searching and introspection by the Christian soldiers of our nation.

What will the spirit of 2026 be?

Will it be laced with animosity and polemics by the soldiers of Christ, or will it be a spirit of care and prayer toward those with whom we disagree? I sincerely hope and pray that it will be the latter. See you at the fireworks!

"Love is patient, love is kind. It does not envy, it does not boast, it is not proud. It is not rude. It is not self-seeking. It is not easily angered. It keeps no account of wrongs. Love takes no pleasure in evil but rejoices in the truth. It bears all things, believes all things, hopes all things, endures all things. Love never fails."
1 Corinthians 13:4-8 (NKJV).

https://washington.org/

BATTLE INDEX

American Revolutionary War

American Civil War

World War II

Vietnam War

The Gulf War (aka Desert Storm)

The War on Terror

Other

SCRIPTURE INDEX

Old Testament

New Testament

ABOUT THE AUTHOR

Blending the author's love of US military history and scripture, Fighting for Life: Forty Reflections from the Trenches" shares extraordinary real-life short stories of soldiers who have faced unimaginable challenges and loss fighting for their lives on the battlefield and in the trenches from the American Revolutionary War to the War on Terror.

McNally offers a powerful collection of forty life lessons with insightful parallels and life-changing truths that give readers the spiritual armor they need to navigate life's challenges on the front lines. Each reflection intertwines gripping true stories of valor, sacrifice, and harrowing experiences.

Tailored for the average Joe, "Fighting for Life" isn't just a book; it's a powerful collection of reflections drawn from the past, providing a lifeline to resilience, purpose, and profound strength for the present.

Whether you're a soldier on active duty, a veteran, or a civilian, you are deployed on today's battlefield of life and will face adversity and challenge. These reflections will inspire you to stand firm in combat, fight with integrity, and emerge victorious while you fight for life, no matter the battlefield.

Made in the USA
Monee, IL
11 June 2025